Phenomenological, Existential, and Humanistic Psychologies

A HISTORICAL SURVEY

Phenomenological, Existential, and Humanistic Psychologies

A HISTORICAL SURVEY

Henryk Misiak, Ph.D.
Fordham University

Virginia Staudt Sexton, Ph.D.
Herbert H. Lehman College
City University of New York

GRUNE & STRATTON
A Subsidiary of Harcourt Brace Jovanovich, Publishers
New York   San Francisco   London

Library of Congress Cataloging in Publication Data
Misiak, Henryk, 1911-
    Phenomenological, existential, and humanistic
psychologies.

    Bibliography: p.
    1. Humanistic psychology. 2. Phenomenological
psychology. 3. Existential psychology. I. Sexton,
Virginia Staudt, joint author. II. Title. [DNLM:
1. Psychological theory—History. BF81 M678p 1973]
BF204.M56 1973   150'.19'2   73-6973
ISBN 0-8089-0814-6

    Grune & Stratton, Inc.
    111 Fifth Avenue
    New York, New York 10003

    Distributed in the United Kingdom by
    Academic Press, Inc. (London) Ltd.
    24/28 Oval Road, London NW1

Library of Congress Catalog Card Number 73-6973
International Standard Book Number 0-8089-0814-6
Printed in the United States of America

Contents

Acknowledgments

We express our thanks to our students whose interest motivated our study and writing, and to many persons who critically reviewed our work. Particularly, we are indebted to those who helped us in collecting information for our book, who responded to our earlier and more recent inquiries, and who served us with their advice: Professors Ewert H. Cousins and J. Quentin Lauer, S. J., of Fordham University; the late Professor Robert B. MacLeod, of Cornell University; Dr. Rollo May; Professors Amedeo Giorgi and Adrian van Kaam, of Duquesne University; Professor Stephan Strasser, of the University of Nijmegen, Holland. We are also grateful for suggestions and assistance in proofreading and index preparation to Professor Richard J. Sexton, of Fordham University; Florence C. Staudt, M.A.; Mary W. Sexton, M.A.; and Richard E. Sexton. We thank Ms. Marilyn Musumeci, M.A., Doctoral Candidate in the Department of Psychology of Fordham University, who helped in the preparation of the manuscript.

Finally, our special thanks go to Messrs. Niels Buessem and the late Frank Kurzer of Grune & Stratton for their encouragement and continued interest in our work.

Henryk Misiak
Virginia Staudt Sexton

Introduction

> Psychology today is torn and riven, and may in fact be said to be three (or more) separate, noncommunicating sciences or groups of scientists. First is the behavioristic, objectivistic, mechanistic, positivistic group. Second is the whole cluster of psychologies that originated in Freud and in psychoanalysis. And third there are the humanistic psychologies, or the "Third Force.". . .
>
> *Abraham H. Maslow (1969)*

In recent years a new movement has emerged on the American psychological scene which has been variably characterized as protest, challenge, complement, extension, or alternative to both behavioristic psychology and psychoanalysis. It has often been called the "Third Force" in American psychology. This movement has gained momentum and an increasing number of adherents among both the young and old generations of psychologists. Although as it grew and spread the movement took on various forms, its principal sources of inspiration have been the phenomenological and existential traditions.

The aims of this book are: (1) to aid the student of psychology in understanding these traditions in their historical context and philosophical foundations; (2) to survey these traditions' expression and effect in contemporary American psychology; and (3) to outline the development, character, and objectives of humanistic psychology, a movement which has relied heavily upon phenomenological and existential thought.

The focus of this book is historical. Its intent is not to evaluate or criticize the movements discussed, although reactions and appraisals by others will be reported. We realize that it is risky, if not foolhardy, to review historically an orientation such as humanistic psychology which appeared in American psychology relatively recently and which is still growing and changing. However, as teachers of history of psychology responding to our students' questions, we felt they could profit from a factual and concise review of this new orientation. Of course, such conciseness has inherent shortcomings, one being an oversimplification of people's thoughts and contributions when presented in summarized versions. Other shortcomings are the necessity for selectivity and inevitable omissions.

Some of the material of this book is borrowed from Chapters 21 and 22 of our earlier work, *History of Psychology: An Overview* (1966). However, the old material has been revised in the light of literature accrued in the interim. The largest part of the present book is devoted to phenomenological philosophy and psychology, as the phenomenological tradition and movement have had the most tangible, the longest, and the widest influence on psychology. This influence can now be examined from a better perspective.

We used primary sources whenever possible but also relied on secondary sources of recognized authority. Particularly helpful were the publications of Herbert Spiegelberg, Professor Emeritus of Philosophy at Washington University in St. Louis, to whom we refer often in the text. After we completed our manuscript, several new relevant books appeared or came to our attention. They could not be considered in the body of our book, but they are included in the bibliography. To facilitate the reader's bibliographical search, we have marked each bibliographical entry at the end of the book with letters: **E** indicates Existential; **G,** General; and **H,** Humanistic. But to avoid an inordinately long bibliography, we usually omitted books cited in the text. They can be located by referring to the Name Index.

1

Phenomenological Philosophy

In the first half of the twentieth century, two new and original philosophical movements appeared: first, phenomenology and second—closely related to phenomenology both historically and conceptually—existentialism. Having developed and spread rapidly, these movements belong now to the most influential philosophies of this century. Their influence transcended philosophy to fields such as literature, art, sociology, law, anthropology, theology, and, notably, psychology and psychiatry.

The effect of these philosophical movements on continental European psychological thought manifested itself in a trend which has been called phenomenological, existential, or phenomenological-existential. The Anglo-American world and its psychology, however, remained indifferent to the phenomenological and existential movements for some time. Finally, in the late 1940s, phenomenological and existential philosophy attracted the attention of some American psychologists. Gradually the phenomenological-existential approach to psychology aroused wider interest, and by the end of the 1950s it had won so much support that some designated it as the "Third Force in American psychology," the two established forces being behaviorism and psychoanalysis. Publications and organized discussions on phenomenology and existentialism reflected this increased interest. In 1959, at the annual convention of the American Psychological Association in Cincinnati, the first American symposium on existential psychology was held. Similar symposia followed in subsequent years. In 1963, a special sym-

1

posium was organized at Rice University under the title "Behaviorism and Phenomenology: Contrasting Bases for Modern Psychology." This meeting signaled that the phenomenological approach had sufficient importance to be confronted with behaviorism. Seven years later, in 1970, an International Symposium on "Phenomenological Psychology: Implications of Phenomenology for Theory and Research" was held at the annual convention of the American Psychological Association in Miami Beach, Florida. Since the phenomenological-existential trend has been of great consequence for psychology on the European continent and has created considerable interest in America, students of psychology will want to understand its meaning and historical development.

David Katz (1950), a prominent European psychologist whose contributions will be discussed in the next chapter, said that "comprehension of contemporary psychology necessitates an understanding of the phenomenological method." The present chapter explains this method and its philosophical basis. Chapter 2 presents the development and application of phenomenology in psychology. The third chapter deals with phenomenological psychology in America, and the fourth with the existential trend in philosophy and psychology and its blending with phenomenology. The fifth chapter discusses the humanistic movement in psychology, a recent brand of psychology which took roots from both phenomenological and existential thought. But since such trends and movements become intelligible only when traced to their philosophical foundations, we shall begin with a brief exposition of these foundations.

EDMUND HUSSERL

The etymology of the term *phenomenology* shows that it is derived from the Greek words *phenomenon* (plural, *phenomena*) and *logos*. *Phenomenon* literally means appearance, that is, that which shows itself. In psychology, phenomena are commonly defined as data of experience which can be observed and described by the experiencing subject at a given time. In philosophy, this word assumes a variety of meanings. In general, however, phenomena mean the appearances of things as contrasted with the things themselves. Kant made this contrast a cornerstone of his philosophy when he taught that our mind cannot ever know the thing itself, or the *noumenon,* as he expressed it, but can only know it as it appears to us, or the *phenomenon.* This theory, which states that our knowledge is restricted to the appearances of things or to phenomena, is called *phenomenalism,* not to be confused with phenomenology.

The term *phenomenology* was coined in the middle of the eighteenth century and subsequently has been used in the history of philosophy to mean different things. Kant, Hegel (who wrote *Phenomenology of Mind,* 1807), Mach, Brentano, and Stumpf—each understood phenomenology in his own way. When Edmund Husserl used this term at the beginning of the twentieth century, he gave it an entirely new meaning and significance. For him, phenomenology was a science of phenomena, that is, of objects as they are experienced or present themselves in our consciousness. Husserl was the founder and most prominent exponent of phenomenology. But it would be wrong to identify all phenomenology of the twentieth century exclusively with his philosophy, as it would be equally wrong, for example, to confine psychoanalysis to the system of Freud. For with the passage of time, various divergent orientations of phenomenology have developed, some of which have gone beyond or even contrary to Husserl's thought. The diversity of phenomenological systems today makes a single general definition of phenomenological philosophy impossible.

Phenomenology is not a school or doctrine in the sense of a body of definite tenets. It is more appropriate to designate it as a movement encompassing various doctrines which have a common core. This common core, or the common denominator that unites the various systems and justifies the phenomenological designation, is its identical point of departure—the phenomenological method. Before describing this method, however, we must first acquaint ourselves with its eminent representative and proponent, Edmund Husserl.

Husserl's Life

Edmund Husserl (1859-1938) was born in Moravia, which was then part of the Austro-Hungarian empire but is now in Czechoslovakia. When Husserl began his academic studies, his main interest lay in mathematics and the natural sciences. He went first to Leipzig, in 1876, where he attended the lectures of Wilhelm Wundt, the founder of experimental psychology. Wundt did not make any special impression on him and in fact was later criticized by him. After two years Husserl went to Berlin, where he studied mainly mathematics. He then traveled to Vienna, where he wrote a dissertation on a mathematical problem and received a Ph.D. in 1883. After serving briefly as an assistant in mathematics at the University of Berlin, he returned to Vienna in 1884 to study philosophy under Franz Brentano (1838-1917).

Brentano was to influence Husserl in more ways than one. It was because of Brentano that Husserl chose philosophy as his lifework.

Moreover, it was Brentano's teaching that fertilized Husserl's mind and directed it to the development of phenomenology. Since Brentano's philosophical ideas were the seed of this new philosophy, Brentano is called the forerunner of the phenomenological movement. Husserl acknowledged his indebtedness to Brentano, referring to him as "my one and only teacher of philosophy." Brentano's personality also had a strong effect on Husserl. Like his master, Husserl felt that he had a mission to fulfill in life. Eventually the two men parted intellectually, for Brentano frowned upon some of Husserl's ideas and perhaps failed to appreciate others; yet they remained friends. Husserl also studied with Brentano's student, Carl Stumpf, in Halle, and their relations were friendly too. In fact, Husserl dedicated his book *Logische Untersuchungen* (*Logical Investigations,* 1900) to Stumpf "in admiration and friendship."

Husserl's academic career in philosophy began at the University of Halle in 1887, when he became a Dozent after completing his qualifying or so-called habilitation thesis on the concept of number. He lectured there for 14 years. In 1901 he moved to the University of Göttingen as an associate professor and remained there for 15 years, until 1916. His colleague at the University was the great pioneer of experimental psychology, Georg E. Müller, who had an active laboratory and whose students also attended Husserl's lectures. Among the Göttingen students, Husserl found followers who formed a special group to discuss phenomenology. A similar group was organized at the University of Munich. Even at this early stage of the phenomenological movement, wide differences among the members of these groups had already emerged.

In 1916 Husserl was appointed full professor at the University of Freiburg in Breisgau, a post he held until his retirement in 1929. During this period and after his retirement as well, he lectured on phenomenology at other universities—in London, Prague, Vienna, and Paris. His assistant in Freiburg was Martin Heidegger, who later became the successor to his post. Husserl died in Freiburg in 1938, at the age of 79. Up to his death, he was active in developing his system. By the time of his death, phenomenology had become a powerful movement, and Husserl had won recognition as one of the keenest intellects and one of the most influential philosophers of the century.

Husserl's Major Works

During his lifetime Husserl published six books. However, he left manuscripts totaling 47,000 pages in shorthand and 12,000 typewritten pages. They were deposited in the Husserl Archives at the University of Louvain in Belgium. Over 20 volumes have been published so far from this material. The New School for Social Research in New York City photocopied Husserl's papers and made them available to scholars in its Husserl Archives, which opened in 1969.

Husserl's early work, *Philosophie der Arithmetik* (*The Philosophy of Arithmetic*, 1891), was not yet explicitly concerned with phenomenology. The beginning of his phenomenological ideas is to be found in the *Logische Untersuchungen*, in two volumes (1900-1901), which was revised and published in three volumes in 1913 (in English, *Logical Investigations*, 1970). The central theme of this work was the foundation of logic. In the book entitled *Ideen zu einer reinen Phänomenologie und phänomenologischen Philosophie* (1913; in English, *Ideas: General Introduction to Pure Phenomenology*, 1931), he presented phenomenology as an objective method to be applied to all philosophy and science. *Vorlesungen zur Phänomenologie des inneren Zeitbewusstseins* (*Lectures on the Phenomenology of Inner Awareness of Time*, 1928) is of particular interest to psychologists studying time perception. The book *Formale und transzendentale Logik* (*Formal and Transcendental Logic*, 1929) and the posthumous *Erfahrung und Urteil* (*Experience and Judgment*, 1939) marked the further development of Husserl's phenomenology. The last book published before his death contained his Paris lectures and appeared first in French as *Méditations cartésiennes* (*Cartesian Meditations*, 1931).

Husserl's Philosophy

In reviewing Husserl's philosophy we shall be selective and mention only those features relevant to the understanding of phenomenological psychology. Therefore, this presentation will include the basic assumptions of phenomenology, the essential characteristics of the phenomenological method, the concept of intentionality, and Husserl's views on psychology.

Husserl's thoughts underwent continuous modification. Historians of the phenomenological movement point to the difference between Husserl's early and later thoughts, particularly to his later novel conceptions which came to light only through posthumous publication of his manuscripts. One of these later concepts was the *Lebenswelt* (the life world, that is, the world of experience of everyday life), which has received considerable attention in contemporary phenomenological and existential writings.

One approach to understanding phenomenology is to view it

with reference to the oldest and most fundamental problem of philosophy: What is the relationship between the objective reality existing outside the mind and the thought which we have of it? How are these two worlds, the world of thought and the world of objective reality, related to each other? All philosophies attempt to answer this question. Phenomenology also made such an attempt. Its points of departure are the affirmations that (1) philosophical inquiry cannot begin with anything else but phenomena of consciousness, since they are the only givens accessible to us, the only material at our immediate disposal; and (2) only phenomena can reveal to us what things, essentially, are. The latter proposition is grounded in the concept of intentionality, which will be explained later. By taking this stand, phenomenology avoids the subject-object dilemma and "the cleavage between subject and object" which, especially since Descartes, "has bedeviled Western thought and science," to use Rollo May's phrase. The only possible approach to the knowledge of things, according to Husserl, is through the exploration of human consciousness. Thus phenomenology is principally a *systematic* and *full* exploration of consciousness.

The phenomena of consciousness are numerous and manifold: things, persons, events, experiences, memories, feelings, moods, thoughts, images, fantasies, mental constructs, and the like. Phenomenology enlists them all and explores them through a method especially adapted for this purpose, known as the *phenomenological method*. Husserl was not its inventor or the first philosopher to employ it. But he refined this method, specified its conditions and object, and raised it to a status of a fundamental philosophical procedure. The method became the keystone of his entire philosophical system. Through its use Husserl hoped to reform philosophy and—this was the guiding motive of Husserl's entire philosophical work—to establish a rigorously scientific philosophy which could provide a firm basis for all other sciences. Husserl's first step in this direction was to demonstrate the fallacy of *psychologism,* a theory which held that mathematics and logic are dependent on psychological laws. Husserl viewed logical laws not as psychological laws or laws contingent on psychological processes, but as self-evident, universal, and eternally true laws.

The Phenomenological Method

The phenomenological method consists of examining whatever is found in consciousness or, in other words, the data or phenomena of consciousness. The method's primary concern is not the act of consciousness, but the object of consciousness—that is, for instance, all that is perceived, imagined, doubted, or loved. The ultimate goal is to reach and grasp the essences of things appearing in consciousness. The method is practiced in a systematic way, proceeding through various steps or techniques. Spiegelberg, in *Phenomenological Movement* (1971), distinguishes seven separate steps in the phenomenological method. Not all of them are used by all phenomenologists. The most fundamental of them, used extensively also by psychologists, is the *phenomenological description*. According to Spiegelberg's interpretation and terminology, three phases of the phenomenological description can be differentiated: *phenomenological intuiting, analyzing,* and *describing.* Intuiting means an intense concentration on, or attentive internal gaze at, the phenomena; analyzing is finding the various constituents of the phenomena and their relationship; describing is an account of the intuited and analyzed phenomena so that they can be understood by others.

Another step of the phenomenological method is called *Wesensschau,* which has been translated from German as *intuition of essences, insight into essences, experience* or *cognition of essences.* Spiegelberg prefers the term "intuiting" to avoid the vague and possibly mystical connotation of "intuition." Intuiting of essences is also called *eidetic intuiting.* The word *eidetic* comes from *eidos,* meaning essence, borrowed by Husserl from Plato. The function of this technique is to seize or apprehend the essences of things through the phenomena. This apprehension is usually accomplished by surveying a series of particular instances exemplifying something more general—as, for instance, surveying various shades of red or colored objects leads to the apprehension of redness or color. Husserl called this procedure of getting to the essences themselves *eidetic reduction.*

The basic prerequisite for the successful practice of the phenomenological method is freeing oneself from any preconceptions or presuppositions. It is imperative that in the exploration of consciousness all biases, theories, beliefs, and habitual modes of thinking be suspended or "bracketed," that is, put between "brackets," as Husserl described it, using an expression familiar in algebra. Husserl called this suspension of all judgments *epoché,* a Greek word meaning abstention. Only when *epoché* is accomplished can fruitful exploration of phenomena be expected, because only then are the phenomena not obscured or distorted by a person's individual idiosyncrasies. *Epoché* is similar in some respects to Cartesian doubt but differs from it in that it never ceases in the phenomenological exploration; it differs also in that the existence of things is not doubted but is simply not considered. This latter characteristic of the *epoché,* that is, the suspension of judgment as to the existence or nonexistence of things, obtains ultimate reduction—the *transcendental reduction,* in which only the stream of pure subjective consciousness is revealed. The phenomena, completely purified, without even the admixture of existential elements, are now ready to be intuited, analyzed, and described. Since transcendental reduction was not sufficiently explained by Husserl, it lent itself to different interpretations and implications, and it is this aspect of Husserl's phenomenology which created deviations from him and dissension among his followers.

The practice of phenomenological method is laborious and requires considerable training. In *Ideas* Husserl stated:

> That we should set aside all previous habits of thought, see through and break down the mental barriers which these habits have set along the horizons of our thinking . . . these are hard demands. . . . To move freely along this new way . . . to learn to see what stands before our eyes, to distinguish, to describe, calls . . . for exacting and laborious studies.

However, whether phenomenological description, so completely devoid of "all previous habits of thought" and prior experiences, is at all feasible has been a question much debated both by phenomenologists and adversaries of phenomenology. Piaget, who believed that intellectual activities of adults are conditioned by earlier forms of behavior, thought this ideal of the phenomenological method unrealizable (1971). He criticized Husserl for neglecting the historical and genetic factors that shape human intellect.

Intentionality

Paramount to the phenomenological theory is the notion of *intentionality.* The reasonableness of phenomenology's goal to get at things themselves through the study of consciousness, as well as phenomenology's claim of the validity of the knowledge thus acquired, rest upon this notion. Husserl learned of intentionality from Brentano, who took it from scholastic philosophy and gave it a new interpretation.

The term *intentionality* comes from the Latin word *intentio* or *intendere,* the latter meaning "to stretch forth." The scholastics—especially Thomas Aquinas—taught that intellect, in the act of cognition of objects, "stretches forth" to the objects and draws them into itself, as it were. Thus the object is said to exist in the mind intentionally; mental phenomena, then, are always related to real objects. Presupposed in this scholastic notion of intentionality is the assertion of the real existence of the physical world. Brentano extended the concept of intentionality to all consciousness and spoke of *intentional inexistence* (in German, *Inexistenz*), which meant existence in or indwelling of the object in consciousness. For Brentano, consciousness is intentional, that is, it always tends to something or has a rapport with the object.

Husserl seized upon Brentano's concept and adapted it to his own thought. For him, as for other phenomenologists, consciousness is always consciousness of something. All the acts of consciousness are naturally related or point to something. There is no love without someone or something loved, no desire without something desired, no perception without something perceived, and so forth. To know the contents of consciousness is to know the object itself. Since the object can be accessible only in consciousness, the sole way to know things is to examine consciousness, for, as Maurice Merleau-Ponty said, the universe resides in consciousness. The purpose of the phenomenological method is to make this examination effective so that we can arrive at the knowledge of things themselves without being entangled in solipsisms.

The concept of intentionality has been analyzed in extensive literature from a variety of standpoints and has been used in various contexts. Rollo May devoted two chapters in *Love and Will* (1969) to intentionality and explained its significance for the psychologist, both scientist and clinician. Van Kaam (1966) sees intentionality as "a fundamental feature of human existence" because, as he says "man *is* a radical or fundamental intentionality directed toward all reality." Intentionality is "the chief determinant of behavior," it manifests itself in behavior, and it is this "intentional behavior" which is "the specific object of the empirical science of psychology."

PHENOMENOLOGY AFTER HUSSERL

Many philosophers were influenced by Husserl as a person and as a philosopher, but few accepted his philosophy to the letter. The phenomenology initiated by him soon broke up into several streams, each following its own course. Husserl's close associate for several years and the expected successor of his philosophical work, Martin Heidegger (b. 1889), departed radically from the master. Although he succeeded Husserl in the chair of philosophy at Freiburg, his philosophy took a new and original direction which eventually became the main inspiration for the existential movement. Heidegger's intellectual estrangement was a painful disappointment to Husserl.

The other most important representative and propagator of the phenomenological movement was Max Scheler (1874-1928). He applied the phenomenological approach to new fields and problems, notably to religion and ethics. There was much vacillation in his views, especially with respect to religion. His deep concern with the human person and human values makes his writings especially interesting to psychologists. One of his books, in English entitled *The Nature of Sympathy,* contains a phenomenological analysis of sympathy, love, and hatred, illustrating the manner in which the phenomenological method can be used in dealing with psychological problems of this nature. In emphasizing the emotional aspects in cognition and interpersonal relations, Scheler moved beyond Husserl. For some, his philosophy became a bridge from phenomenology to existentialism.

The phenomenological movement, confined at first mostly to Germany, penetrated into France where it soon showed a new vigor and began to merge with the existential current. The most prominent representatives of this development, about whom more will be said in Chapter 4, were Gabriel Marcel, Jean-Paul Sartre, Paul Ricoeur, and Maurice Merleau-Ponty. In almost every European country phenomenology found interpreters and followers, some closer to, others more distant from, the Husserlian phenomenology. Phenomenological societies and study circles were organized. In Britain, for example, the Society for Phenomenology was formed, with its own journal. Some non-German phenomenologists carried phenomenology to heretofore unexplored territories and ventured syntheses of phenomenology with other philosophical currents. One of the original and intriguing examples is the Polish philosopher Roman Ingarden (b. 1893), Husserl's student, who remained in touch with his master through extensive correspondence and study of his newly published works. But in Ingarden's own development—mostly through an analysis of art—he moved away from the idealism of phenomenology toward realism. A philosopher of high rank, Ingarden is only beginning to be better known and appreciated partly because a significant portion of his major work, *The Controversy Over the Existence of the World* (two volumes, 1946-1948), was translated into English (*Time and Modes of Being,* 1964) and other languages. Most of Ingarden's works, however, are still not available to non-Polish readers.

Phenomenology in America

While phenomenology was growing and winning new adherents in continental Europe, it was little known in America. Husserl's works were not available in English translation, with the exception of the *Ideas,* which appeared in 1931 translated by an Australian scholar, and there were few studies before that date. Only in the later 1930s did Americans who had studied philosophy in Europe and European phenomenologists who immigrated to America begin to acquaint the American public with phenomenology. An American pioneer in bringing Husserl to the attention of the public in this country was the philosopher Marvin Farber (b. 1901). Farber was Husserl's student, on whose initiative an International Phenomenological Society was organized in 1939 and a quarterly, *Philosophy and Phenomenological Research,* was founded in 1940. This journal, although not confined solely to phenomenology, has been the main platform for discussions on phenomenological philosophy in this country. Farber edited a book of essays on Husserl in 1940 and published his own work on Husserl's phenomenology, *The Foundation of Phenomenology,* in 1943 (2nd ed., 1962). The latter book was the first extensive exposition of Husserl's phenomenology in America. Although sympathetic to Husserl's philosophy, Farber was never entirely committed to it and remained critical of some of its aspects.

There have been several other Americans who interpreted phenomenology and sometimes translated Husserl's works into English. Among them was Dorion Cairns (1901-1973), who spent several years in Freiburg in close contact with Husserl. Cairns's 1939 article, *Results of Husserl's Investigations,* was one of the earliest and most concise introductions to Husserl in America. In 1960 he translated Husserl's *Cartesianische Meditationes* (written in 1931, published posthumously in 1950; in English, *Cartesian Meditations*). J. Quentin Lauer (b. 1917) gave a comprehensive presentation of Husserl's phenomenological philosophy in his book, *The Triumph of Subjectivity,* in 1958. He published an English translation of Husserl's two short works, with an introduction and notes, under the title *Phenomenology and the Crisis of Philosophy* (1965). John Wild (1901-1972), a well-known American philosopher who spent some time in Freiburg in 1931 and studied with Heidegger, had a lively interest in phenomenology and existentialism and published works sympathetic to both movements. At his initiative the Society for Phenomenology and Existential Philosophy was organized in 1962. Several European exponents of phenomenology who settled in America initiated new directions in phenomenological research. Among them were Alfred Schuetz (1899-1959), who applied phenomenology to social problems; Aron Gurwitsch (b. 1901), whose interest has been the field of consciousness; Dietrich von Hildebrand (b. 1889), who published works on ethics and religious values; and Herbert Spiegelberg (b. 1904), a prominent historian of the phenomenological movement.

In 1960 Spiegelberg published a two-volume work, *The Phenomenological Movement,* which he revised in 1965 and added supplementary material in 1971. This book is the most competent and extensive survey and evaluation of phenomenology; it is also a rich source of bibliographical information. Spiegelberg was born in Strasbourg and studied in Heidelberg, Freiburg (1924-1925), and Munich. He immigrated to the United States in 1938. He has been professor of philosophy at Washington University in St. Louis, and in addition to his historical works he has published phenomenological studies. His most recent work is *Phenomenology in Psychology and Psychiatry: A Historical Introduction* (1972a). This thorough, scholarly, and insightful opus will undoubtedly be an important reference for historians of psychology and for those interested in phenomenological psychology and psychiatry.

HUSSERL AND PSYCHOLOGY

The issue of psychology and the place to be assigned to psychology in the phenomenological system occupied Husserl seriously all his life. He was convinced that psychology was an important discipline to which phenomenology could and should contribute much, but from which phenomenology could also derive considerable benefits. His views on this matter underwent substantial evolution, as he himself admitted and as he admonished those who did not keep up with his progression.

Husserl was familiar with the new psychology of his day, especially with German and Austrian psychology. He referred to this psychology as *empirical,* which he conceived as a positive science (*positive Wissenschaft*), distinguished from the older philosophical psychology and his own phenomenological psychology (which was *eine Erfahrungswissenschaft*). We remember that he knew Wilhelm Wundt, studied under Brentano, was a friend of Carl Stumpf, and was a colleague of G. E. Müller at Göttingen University. He read William James and was favorably impressed, was acquainted with the writings of Theodore Lipps, and also knew at least some of the works of the Würzburg and Gestalt schools. However, Husserl's attitude toward leading contemporary psychologists and psychological schools was in general critical, and personal relations with them were far from affectionate. He admitted that he could not follow psychological literature. Indeed, there is no evidence that Husserl was familiar with experimental psychology of the 1920s and 1930s outside Germany.

Husserl's intent was to bridge empirical psychology with phenomenology by developing a new and special psychological discipline which he called at first *rational psychology* and *eidetic psychology* and later termed *phenomenological psychology*. His lecture courses in 1925 and 1928, published posthumously by W. Biemel in 1962 as *Phänomenologische Psychologie,* and also his other works dealt with the nature of this newly conceived discipline. The goal of this psychology was to study consciousness in its meaningful structure and function. Such a study, oriented and leading toward transcendental phenomenology, also provided a justification and basis for empirical psychology, as well as a methodology for the exploration of consciousness. Experimentation could be practiced as an aid and complement to phenomenological investigation. The phenomenological method used in psychological inquiries, Husserl conceded, need not be as radical in its reduction as that used in transcendental phenomenology. Moreover, by accepting the view that in man the psychological and the physiological are always connected, Husserl recognized *psycho-physical psychology* as a study of psychic life manifested in bodily functions and overt behavior. But he was opposed to accounting for psychic life exclusively in terms of bodily events or to reducing psychic life to bodily manifestations. It is clear that Husserl was as opposed to the positivistic and mechanistic tendencies in psychology as he was to the other extreme, psychologism. Also irreconcilable with his view was the empiricist and associationist notion of consciousness.

In Joseph Kockelmans's opinion (1971), "Husserl's greatest contribution to the sciences of man in general and to psychology in particular has been the opening up of new possibilities." For example, Husserl pointed out that (1) a strict empirical psychology was possible and necessary, and that (2) "a mere investigation of facts alone does not yet yield scientific, psychological knowledge, even if such an investigation is in continuous harmony with immediately given phenomena." Psychology, Kockelmans argued, "cannot be merely a collection of correlated facts," but must also be concerned "with discovering the genuine meaning which is found in all forms of our orientation towards the world. And it is precisely in this realm that the task of a phenomenological . . . psychology is to be found." This role of phenomenology, however, was not immediately apparent to psychologists of Husserl's time.

Husserl's Influence on His Contemporary Psychologists

When psychologists in Germany, Austria, and other countries became better acquainted with Husserl's works, they began to react to them—some favorably, others negatively. Wilhelm Wundt, whom Husserl criticized for his alleged psychologism, was impressed by neither Husserl nor his phenomenology, which he regarded as scholastic philosophy. Edward B. Titchener (1867-1927) made a genuine effort to understand Husserl. A British psychologist who was the most eminent representative of Wundtian psychology and who came to America to Cornell University in 1893, Titchener became the founder and leader of the school of structuralism. In 1912 he declared that "no form of phenomenology . . . can be truly scientific." Realizing Husserl's "profound influence upon current psychological thought," Titchener decided in 1917 to study Husserl "less for his own sake, than for the way in which psychologists have understood him." In his *Systematic Psychology: Prolegomena* (1929), published posthumously, Titchener displayed familiarity with Husserl's major books and discussed their influence on German and Austrian psychology. He himself did not find reasons to alter his original position regarding the value of Husserl's phenomenology for psychology. Nevertheless Titchener, impressed by the success of the Gestaltists and experimental phenomenology, later allowed his students to try "phenomenologizing," and some phenomenological descriptions were applied at the Cornell laboratory.

In Göttingen, where Husserl lectured for 15 years (1901-1916), Georg E. Müller (1850-1934) was professor and director of an active psychological laboratory, second in prominence and influence only to Wundt's laboratory in Leipzig. The ways of these two men "lay worlds apart," according to Carl Spearman, eminent British psychologist who spent some time in Göttingen. "In fact," Spearman wrote, "the sole thing that seemed common to the two was the inability of each to appreciate the other." But some of Müller's students did appreciate Husserl and fell under his spell, as will be seen later.

In general, the younger generation of psyhcologists in Germany and Austria in the the first two decades of this century responded to Husserl more favorably than their teachers had, as did the students from other countries taking their degrees at German universities. Phenomenological description and analysis, acquired from Brentano, Stumpf, or Husserl, found wide acceptance among European experimental psychologists. Many studies in the psychological laboratories at Göttingen and Würzburg, another center of psychological research and training under the direction of Oswald Külpe (1862-1915), owed their inspiration to Husserl. Karl Bühler (1879-1963), who was later to be a leading figure in Austrian psychology and an influential writer, was much impressed by Husserl, and this was undoubtedly a factor in his interest in and research on thought processes at Würzburg (1907-1908). Boring (1950) thought that Bühler might even have introduced Husserl's philosophy to Külpe, who later showed such a vivid interest in phenomenology as to make Titchener (1929) remark that how deeply Husserl "affected the psychology of Külpe himself, we shall probably never know." Titchener also thought that the book *Psychologie* (1914) by one of the members of the Würzburg school, August Messer, "was largely shaped" by Husserl. Husserl's influence reached psychologists at other German universities such as Munich, Frankfurt, Berlin, and Hamburg. It was the psychologists of this generation, immigrating to the United States in the 1930s, who introduced American psychologists to phenomenology and who later helped the formation of the "Third Force" in American psychology.

Gestalt Psychology

Gestalt psychology, a new psychological school which arose in Germany in 1911 when Husserl was already well-known and which stressed the phenomenological approach, could have been expected to ally itself with the Husserlian phenomenology. However, while this school was also a rebellion against the dominant psychology, the atomistic Wundtian psychology, just as phenomenology was a revolt against the prevailing philosophy, Gestalt psychology developed independently of Husserl. The founders of the Gestalt system, Wertheimer, Koffka, and Köhler, were exposed to the phenomenological tradition of Ewald Hering, Brentano, and Stumpf; they no doubt knew of Husserl and perhaps met him personally. Yet they were not particularly interested in the phenomenology of Husserl: apparently they did not find it relevant to their theory. Only in America in the late 1920s did the Gestaltists begin to make explicit references to Husserl. Aron Gurwitsch, who studied Gestalt psychology and recognized its closeness to phenomenology, has been credited with making the Gestaltists more aware of Husserlian phenomenology. Köhler respected phenomenological psychology and publicly recognized its contributions, but he developed his own philosophical views independently of Husserl. Referring to Husserl in 1944, Köhler was explicit in distinguishing his phenomenology from Husserl's. He expressed concern whether the Husserlian brackets in the phenomenological analysis may not "sooner or later turn out to be weapons of an ontological prejudice. . . . In fact," he continued, "I am not sure whether Husserl himself has not used them as such weapons."

EVALUATION

Historians of philosophy agree that Husserl's phenomenology was a decisive break from the philosophical past and that it has affected not only philosophy but also other domains of thought. The intention of phenomenology was to provide a methodology which would serve all fields of inquiry. According to Anna-Teresa Tymieniecka's *Phenomenology and Science in Contemporary European Thought* (1962), the phenomenological method has been adopted by almost all European philosophers and has been successfully applied to various subject matters. Phenomenology has profoundly affected psychology, both in theory and in practice. Its influence on psychology will be discussed more explicitly in the following chapters.

The English-speaking world, whose philosophical thought has followed the naturalistic, neopositivistic, and analytical trend, was at first not receptive to phenomenology. To the American mind, phenomenology appeared too ambiguous and too speculative to be of any significant value in science—psychology included. Gradually interest in phenomenology in America has grown and literature on phenomenological problems has increased. Departments of philosophy at American universities have introduced courses in phenomenological philosophy. At present there is hardly any major American university without at least one phenomenologist on its philosophical faculty.

Phenomenology's role in philosophy and science has not ended. It appears that this philosophy is able to cope with several problems of growing concern to both philosophers and scientists. One of these problems is the question and development of a viable system of values for the survival of mankind, a problem now often discussed within the scientific community in America. Since the world of values has been an area of intensive study by many phenomenologists, one can expect that the present need for a better system of values will stimulate further contributions by phenomenologists.

SUMMARY

We reviewed phenomenological philosophy and the contributions, especially to psychology, of its founder, Edmund Husserl. The following is a brief recapitulation of the main points discussed in the text. The chart illustrates the influence of Husserl and names some representatives of phenomenology.

Phenomenological Philosophy

Precursor: Franz Brentano (1838-1917)
Founder and principal exponent: Edmund Husserl (1859-1938)
Definition: Phenomenology in a broad sense is a philosophy which advocates Husserl's motto "going to the things themselves" ("zu den Sachen selbst"), conceived as a faithful and unbiased description of the givens of consciousness. Thus phenomenology is principally a method of: (a) direct intuition as the primary source of knowledge; (b) intuitive study of essences. This method is adopted by various philosophical orientations which are collectively referred to as the *Phenomenological Movement.*

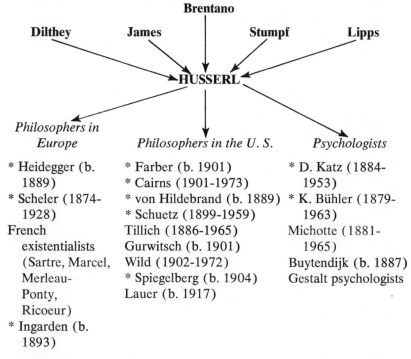

Brentano

Dilthey   James   Stumpf   Lipps

HUSSERL

Philosophers in Europe	*Philosophers in the U. S.*	*Psychologists*
* Heidegger (b. 1889)	* Farber (b. 1901)	* D. Katz (1884-1953)
* Scheler (1874-1928)	* Cairns (1901-1973)	* K. Bühler (1879-1963)
French existentialists (Sartre, Marcel, Merleau-Ponty, Ricoeur)	* von Hildebrand (b. 1889)	Michotte (1881-1965)
	* Schuetz (1899-1959)	
	Tillich (1886-1965)	Buytendijk (b. 1887)
	Gurwitsch (b. 1901)	Gestalt psychologists
	Wild (1902-1972)	
* Ingarden (b. 1893)	* Spiegelberg (b. 1904)	
	Lauer (b. 1917)	

Psychologists Who Influenced Husserl, and Philosophers and Psychologists Whom Husserl Influenced. (Asterisks indicate those who studied with Husserl or were associated with him at some time.)

SUGGESTED READINGS

A clear, readable introduction to philosophical phenomenology which should be particularly meaningful to psychologists is:

Zaner, R. M. *The way of phenomenology: Criticism as a philosophical discipline.* New York: Pegasus, 1970.

Selection of excerpts from major works in phenomenology and existentialism, with informative introductions:

Solomon, R. C. (Ed.) *Phenomenology and existentialism.* New York: Harper & Row, 1972.

The most extensive and authoritative history of the phenomenological movement is:

Spiegelberg, H. *The phenomenological movement.* (2nd ed.; 3rd impression) The Hague: Nijhoff, 1971. 2 vols.

The best account of Husserl's phenomenological psychology to date is:

Kockelmans, J. J. *Edmund Husserl's phenomenological psychology: A historico-critical study.* Pittsburgh: Duquesne University Press, 1967.

2

Phenomenological Psychology

Before the connection between phenomenology and psychology is discussed, one common misconception must be dispelled: namely, that phenomenology in psychology has resulted solely from Husserl's influence or that it is directly a product of phenomenological philosophy. As much as it is true that Husserl profoundly influenced psychology, the phenomenological approach in psychology existed long before him. What Merleau-Ponty observed about phenomenological philosophy can also be applied to phenomenological psychology. "The opinion of the responsible philosopher must be," he said, "that phenomenology can be practiced and identified as a manner or style of thinking, that it existed as a movement before arriving at complete awareness of itself as a philosophy." The phenomenological approach in psychology existed before it crystallized into the form which we now call phenomenological psychology. This chapter is about the development and manifestations of this approach in psychology.

The most frequent terms denoting the relation between phenomenology and psychology have been *phenomenological psychology* and *psychological phenomenology*. It is with the distinction and definition of these terms that we shall begin.

PSYCHOLOGICAL PHENOMENOLOGY

The term *psychological phenomenology* refers to phenomenology as a method applied to psychological problems or employed at the psychological level of inquiry. In this context, *psychological phenomenology* is to be distinguished from *philosophical* or *transcendental phenomenology*, which, as noted in Chapter 1, is a procedure of philosophy directed toward the essences of things and the knowledge of ultimate reality. Psychological phenomenology is a more restricted and specific procedure designed to explore man's immediate consciousness and experience. It may be defined as a systematic observation and description of the experience of a conscious individual in a given situation. Karl Jaspers defined it as "the completest and most careful description possible of what is experienced by healthy or by sick people." The exploration of consciousness refers both to acts and contents of consciousness and to their objects and meanings. The phenomenal data to be explored include perceptions, feelings, images, memories, ideas, and everything else that appears in consciousness. These data are accepted and described as they are experienced without any presuppositions or transformations. Past knowledge, modes of thinking, and theoretical biases must be kept in abeyance or "bracketed out," as the phenomenologists would say, in order to view the phenomenal world in all its richness and purity. Robert B. MacLeod calls this "an attitude of disciplined naïveté."

Phenomenology and Introspection

Psychological phenomenology is different from the classical introspection of Wundt and Titchener in many respects. In fact, phenomenologists attacked introspection as a biased and only fragmentary exploration of consciousness. Wolfgang Köhler, the Gestaltist, voiced the phenomenologists' criticism in *Gestalt Psychology* (1929), pointing out the limitations and weaknesses of introspection as a method in psychology.

In classical introspection, a well-trained observer, upon receiving a stimulus, relates his impressions and attempts to reduce them to the simplest mental elements, that is, to sensations, feelings, images. He also attempts to find their attributes, such as quality, intensity, and duration. In a phenomenological study, no assumption concerning the composition or attributes of impressions is allowed. Moreover, whereas in an introspective report objects and meanings are excluded, in a phenomenological study they are essential. The phenomenologist is interested in the meaning that stimuli or situations have for the observer. Presented with a tactual stimulus—for example, a sheet of paper—Titchener's subject was not asked what the object was. Rather, he was asked to analyze his impressions in terms of the classical fourfold elements of touch, namely pain, warmth, cold, and pressure, and to report any other sensory elements that might have been experienced, such as kinesthetic sensation. In a phenomenological experiment the subject reports, in a similar situation, that the presented stimulus is a sheet of paper, if he had so identified it, and that it feels smooth or rough, hard or soft, large or small.

A good example of the contrast in methodology and results is found by comparing the experiments performed by Titchener's students at Cornell University on so-called touch blends with the phenomenological studies of touch by David Katz (1925) and Géza Révész (1938). In his study in 1933, Zigler, Titchener's student, who was interested in determining the sensory components of clamminess, found that it could be reduced to cold, softness, movement, and unpleasant imagery. Katz's studies of tactual impressions concentrated not on the combination of the sensory elements but on the richness of tactual experiences. The studies revealed different modes of appearances of touches. Katz was able to classify these modes into several meaningful categories.

Titchener, writing on introspection in 1912, referred to phenomenology and conceded that a phenomenological account may be "useful or even necessary as the starting-point of a truly psychological description" or "as an additional check" after the introspective description, but that in itself a phenomenological account had no scientific value. However, phenomenologists proved so successful in the use of their method, through which they made numerous contributions to the field of sensation, perception, and other fields, that by 1930 the phenomenological method had virtually displaced introspection.

Phenomenological Tradition

Examples of a phenomenological approach can be found in all periods of the history of psychology. An early outstanding example of this approach is the fourth-century autobiography, the *Confessions,* in which its author, St. Augustine (354-430), bishop of Hippo, gives a deep and sincere account of his experiences, emotions, memories, desires, and other feelings and thoughts. Many contemporary phenomenological writings refer to St. Augustine and quote him. Husserl himself, in his lecture in Paris, cited St. Augustine's statement, "Turn into yourself: truth dwells inside man."

In the seventeenth century, Descartes began his philosophical quest with doubt, resolved in the celebrated *Cogito, ergo sum,* as a basis of his philosophy. His radical dualism and his psychology built on the assumption of a dichotomy of the thinking mind and the mechanical body favored the phenomenological method as appropriate for the study of a spiritual entity, the mind. Being a psychology of mind, Cartesian psychology fostered and strengthened the phenomenological approach. Consequently the phenomenologists of the twentieth century have discussed Cartesian philosophy extensively. Descartes has been the reference point with which they contrast or compare their own views.

The first systematic and effective use of phenomenological description was in the study of visual phenomena. The studies of Goethe and Purkinje at the beginning of the nineteenth century are often cited for their use of the phenomenological method in this field. Goethe systematically and detailedly studied many subjective color phenomena, among them afterimages and effects of contrasts on color perception. His investigations and the rich inventory of various color phenomena were described by him in his two-volume *Zur Farbenlehre* (*On Colors,* 1810). After Goethe, many other distinguished investigators, including Hering, Stumpf, G. E. Müller, David Katz, Wertheimer, Ach, and Michotte, pursued studies of various sensory and perceptual phenomena. Whereas Goethe mistrusted experimentation and obstinately rejected experimental evidence in favor of purely phenomenological verification, his successors in these investigations undertook laboratory experimentation and used experimental data. These data complemented phenomenological observations and were related to data of physics and physiology. Such constructs as "color solid," "smell prism," and "taste tetrahedron" are products of phenomenological research of this kind.

Although in the second half of the nineteenth century the emphasis in sensory and perceptual research shifted to physiological and psychophysical aspects, phenomenological studies continued. Prominent physiologists and psychophysicists—among them Johannes Müller and Gustav T. Fechner—also conducted phenomenological studies. Ewald Hering, particularly, made extensive use of phenomenology in his studies of vision and based his theories, which clashed with those of Helmholtz, on phenomenological material. The Hering-Helmholtz controversy illustrates the two approaches—experimental and phenomenological—with their merits and shortcomings. Stumpf, who practiced both approaches in his studies of tones, regarded phenomenology as a preparatory stage of psychology and for this reason called it the "propaedeutics" of psychology. An example of an early phenomenological psychology, independent of Husserl but allied to Brentano's phenomenology, is found in Alexander Pfänder (1870-1941), professor at the University of Munich. Although he did not develop a full system of phenomenological psychology, Pfänder applied the phenomenological approach to several psychological problems such as perception, willing, motivation, and emotions. His major original work, *Phenomenology of Willing,* appeared in 1900.

EXPERIMENTAL PHENOMENOLOGY

At the beginning of the twentieth century, the scope of phenomenological research was extended to other problems. The Würzburg and Göttingen laboratories studied learning, thought, and will. The French used the phenomenological method in their studies of affective states and psychopathological conditions. Ribot's study of the experiences involved in mechanical invention was also principally phenomenological. Finally Katz and Wertheimer inaugurated a new era of phenomenological psychology when they launched their systematic experimentation on, respectively, color perception and apparent movement. Their research incorporated both the phenomenological method and laboratory techniques—a combination which has been called *experimental phenomenology.* The findings obtained through this new methodology provided the basis for the Gestalt school. The success of this school in the psychology of perception was largely due to its skillful use of experimental phenomenology. It gained new adherents to phenomenology and inspired further phenomenologically oriented research, especially in continental Europe, where the phenomenological tradition was stronger than in America or England. Husserl's philosophy gave an identity, name, and a philosophical justification and framework to this already existing and receptive phenomenological approach in psychology. It also reinforced it and occasionally inspired new areas of inquiry.

David Katz

In the twentieth century, experimental phenomenology found its first prominent exponent in David Katz (1884-1953). The contributions which he made to this field during a scientific career spanning more than half a century exemplify the phenomenological-experimental trend at its best. Three influences interacted in the formation of David Katz as a phenomenologist and psychologist: the phenomenological tradition represented by Hering, Husserl's phenomenology, and the experimental spirit of the Göttingen laboratory. Katz was interested in Hering's work and theories, visited Hering's laboratory at

Leipzig, and later, after his own investigations, sent Hering his book on color perception, which evoked favorable comment from Hering. Regarding Husserl, Katz stated in his autobiography,

> To me phenomenology, as advocated . . . by Edmund Husserl, seemed to be the most important connection between philosophy and psychology. None of my academic teachers with the exception of G. E. Müller has more deeply influenced my method of work and my attitude in psychological matters than Husserl by his phenomenological method.

For 14 years, Husserl and Katz were at the same university. Husserl took "an ardent interest," as Katz said, in his work on color and touch. Max Scheler, who became Katz's friend, was also interested in his research. Stumpf, too, showed much concern with Katz's academic career. Katz was associated for 18 years with the Göttingen laboratory, known for its strong experimental orientation. He studied at Göttingen, received his Ph.D. degree there in 1906, and from 1907 to 1919 was Müller's assistant. Katz's wife, who later collaborated with him on several research projects, was a former Göttingen student.

With this background of phenomenology—the old (Hering) and the new (Husserl)—and excellently trained in experimental methods, Katz was well prepared to become the best exponent and promoter of phenomenological psychology. Another factor in his serious engagement with this psychology was his interest in the Gestalt school and his "cordial relations," as he termed them, with its members and sympathizers. His highly successful book *Gestalt Psychology* (1943) was a concise, clear appraisal of the school. In its preface he declared that although his "views are close to those of the Gestalt psychologists in many, perhaps even in most respects," he does "not agree with them completely" and does "not believe that all psychological facts are in accord with the Gestalt viewpoint." In addition to this volume, Katz wrote *Der Aufbau der Tastwelt* (*The World of Touch,* 1925), *Gespräche mit Kindern* (1927; English translation, *Conversations with Children,* 1936) in collaboration with his wife, *Hunger und Appetit* (*Hunger and Appetite,* 1932), and the book best known in American circles, *The World of Colour* (published in English in 1935 from a 1930 German edition). He also published numerous articles and monographs on topics related mostly to his experimental research.

Katz left Göttingen in 1919 to become professor in Rostock, remaining there until 1933 when the Nazis made his stay impossible because of his non-Aryan origin. He left Germany and went to England, where he conducted research for four years until he was called to a professorship in Stockholm. Katz was a visiting professor in the United States in 1929 and in 1950.

Katz's Phenomenological Research

The phenomenological approach, which Katz pursued all his life, manifested itself in his first published research on children's drawings in 1906, where he touched upon the phenomenon of color constancy, that is, the persistence of colors despite a change in illumination. Later he studied this phenomenon more extensively. Troubled by the paucity of psychological treatment of visual phenomena compared to the abundance of physiological studies, and complaining that the latter—frequently conducted by psychologists—"could be handled just as well or even better by a sensory physiologist," he started research on the psychology of color. This research, done in 1911, preceded Wertheimer's discovery of the *phi* phenomenon and is cited as the beginning of experimental phenomenology. It was continued and culminated in the publication of *The World of Colour*. Through skillful experiments, Katz demonstrated for the first time new and up to then unknown or unexplored color phenomena. His results proved convincingly that simple attributes of hue, brightness, and saturation are inadequate to account for all color experiences, and that it is necessary to go beyond the dimensions related to the physical properties of the stimulus. The same color can appear, Katz found, in different modes such as a surface color, or film color, or as bulky, shiny, transparent, or luminous—categories now well-known to students of color. Katz showed that the chromatic or achromatic objects tend to be perceived as the same color even when their illumination changes. Equally, the normal apparent brightness of the objects tends to remain the same, even if the intensity of their illumination is increased or decreased. For example, the whiteness of a sheet of paper is perceived to be the same in spite of dimmer or brighter light falling on the paper. This constancy of color or brightness is destroyed if the observer views the object isolated from the rest of the visual field and is thereby deprived of certain cues. This is the case when the object is observed through a "reduction screen," that is, a small hole. This finding demonstrated the effect of the total field in the perceptual process. Katz's subsequent studies amplified many of his findings and substantiated his theoretical views.

It was characteristic of Katz to be fascinated by unexplored fields and to venture into them with enthusiasm. Some areas of research charted by him are still waiting to be pursued further. He moved from the exploration of color phenomena to tactual sensations, from problems of child psychology to the study of animal behavior, and from the psychology of mathematics instruction to the psychology of hunger and appetite. His studies included such divergent areas as proprioception, taste, vibratory sense, formation of composite photographs, temporal measurement of phases of writing, drug effects, and even occult phenomena. In the last decade of his life he became seriously interested in the reaction of the human and animal organism to exceptional conditions. Averse to laboratory experimentation of trivial and superficial matters, which in his opinion produces little meaningful information for psychology despite the expenditure of much time and energy, Katz preferred to concentrate on processes basic to understanding the organism.

Katz is considered the first experimentalist who systematically and consistently applied the phenomenological method to a wide array of psychological problems. He was able to collect rich, experimentally sound data which challenged the atomistic and associationistic viewpoints. He also demonstrated the value of the holistic approach in psychological investigations and the need to consider the dynamic interplay between environmental and subjective variables in understanding perception and adaptive responses. His work generated much interest in continental Europe and found followers in many laboratories.

Other Phenomenologists

Phenomenological research similar to Katz's was often instituted in European laboratories by students from Göttingen and Würzburg. The Danish psychologist Edgar Rubin, known for his research on figure and ground, pursued this course in Copenhagen; Géza Révész did the same in his native Hungary; Narziss Ach in Königsberg; Karl Bühler in Vienna; Gemelli in Milan; and Michotte in Louvain. Their students, when appointed to chairs and laboratories, extended the phenomenological spirit to new places. The two founders of Gestalt psychology, Wertheimer and Koffka, were students at Würzburg, and Wertheimer received his Ph.D. under Külpe. Much research in Germany from 1910 to 1940 was phenomenological, often stimulated by problems posed by the Gestalt school. In addition to the Berlin school where Gestalt psychology flourished, another prominent center of phenomenological research continued at Göttingen. Leipzig became the third center when Wundt's successor, Felix Krueger, turned to the study of personality and emotions. Although perception had the largest share in these investigations, other areas were also intensively explored, such as volition, thought, expressions, esthetics, and language. New problems were constantly being added to the repertoire of phenomenological studies. It must be noted, however, that phenomenology, while the major single force in European psychology from 1910 to 1940, also found strong critics and opponents in Germany and elsewhere.

But the phenomenological trend was not confined exclusively to experimentation; it also expressed itself in theory. The data continually amassed demanded a theoretical framework which would structure and render the data meaningful. Several theories on emotions, personality, and adjustment, conceived in Europe, bear the phenomenological trademark. Continental European psychologists develop hypotheses and theories which frequently are based on or supported by evidence too scanty to convince their American colleagues. These theories are, however, often effective as a motivating drive and a guiding principle in research.

Among the outstanding European phenomenological psychologists, two have gained particular renown: a Belgian, Albert Michotte, for his systematic experimental studies; and a Dutchman, F. J. J. Buytendijk, chiefly for his theoretical contributions. Both were influenced directly by Husserl, but Buytendijk, more than Michotte, worked in continued close association with phenomenological and existential thought. A unique position in contemporary phenomenology is held by the French philosopher Maurice Merleau-Ponty, once professor of child psychology at the Sorbonne. He effected a confrontation of psychological and philosophical problems within the phenomenological framework and discussed those problems systematically in two books, one on perception, the other on behavior. The works of some British psychologists in the 1920s and 1930s were phenomenological in character. Honoria Wells's *The Phenomenology of Acts of Choice* (1927) can be cited as an example.

Albert Edouard Michotte

Born in Brussels, Albert Edouard Michotte van den Berck (1881-1965) studied at the University of Louvain. He also worked at the Leipzig and Würzburg laboratories. In 1905 he started his teaching career at the University of Louvain, with which he was associated until his retirement in 1946. An avid and skillful experimentalist, Michotte devoted his best efforts to the Louvain laboratory, which he directed for 25 years. Students from many countries studied and conducted research under him. A strong believer in the value of scientific "cross-stimulation," as he called it, he maintained lively contacts with psychologists in many countries and attended international congresses of psychology. He served as president of the International Union of Scientific Psychology and the Fifteenth International Congress of Psychology in 1957. Michotte won admiration, respect, and friendship to a rare degree from students and colleagues for his work and personal qualities.

Three periods can be distinguished in Michotte's research career: from 1905 to 1914, from 1920 to 1939, and from 1939 to his death. In the first period, the research was similar to that of the Würzburg school in that it focused on volition. The second period included problems of perception, movement, rhythm, and learning. The investigations after 1939 on the perception of causality were the most original and attracted the widest attention. New ingenious experimental techniques were used for the first time in these studies. The experiments consisted of observing the relations of moving objects and describing the observers' impressions. In one series of experiments, circular spots were projected on the screen and made to move. In a variation of this series, object A moved toward object B, and when both were joined, A was stopped and B moved in the direction of A's previous motion. The impression of all the observers was that A gave impulse to, or hurled, B. In another variation, A, after having approached B, continued to move together with B. In this case the observers had the impression that A carried, pushed, or took away B with itself. In a different series of experiments, rectangles were moved along a horizontal slot at various speeds and in different relative positions. The spatial and temporal parameters determining the impressions reported by the observers were systematically explored. The methods and results of the experiments were first described in Michotte's 1946 book (in French; 2nd ed. in 1954). Its second edition appeared in 1963 in English, with a chapter added by the author as *Perception of Causality*. David Katz said that this book is "not only one of the most important contributions to experimental psychology in recent years, it will take its place among the classical works of psychology."

From his research, Michotte concluded that the perception of causality is like any other perception, such as that of color or tone. It is a primary experience, not a secondary interpretation of experience, and has a quality of a Gestalt, similar to the *phi* phenomenon, occurring invariably under certain conditions. Further experiments on causality and allied problems conducted in the 1940s and 1950s provided additional information about these perceptual phenomena. This phase of experimentation was presented by Michotte and several of his collaborators in a volume published on his 80th birthday, *Causalité, permanence et réalité phénoménales (Phenomenal Causality, Perma-*

nence and Reality, 1962). In his analysis of the perceptual phenomena of causality, Michotte was careful to specify that this was mechanical causality, thereby avoiding a commitment to any philosophical theory of causality.

This extensive research on causality and related problems, conducted at Louvain for over 25 years, constitutes a significant chapter of phenomenological psychology. "To our scientific knowledge of the construction of this phenomenal world," as Nuttin expressed it (1966), "Michotte brought an original and important contribution." Although Michotte has been linked with either the Gestalt school or the school of functionalism, he and his research cannot be categorized in terms of schools. Michotte, opposed to theoretical biases, remained free from school bonds and was primarily concerned with giving full and impartial attention to the phenomena themselves. This does not mean that Michotte was not interested in theoretical issues or in the theoretical implications of his experimental findings. However, he preferred to give priority to experimentation rather than to theorizing.

Many of Michotte's students from his long teaching career have attained prominence in psychology. Among them are Joseph Nuttin (b. 1909), who became Michotte's successor at Louvain University; Georges Thines (b. 1923), professor at Louvain and co-editor of the *Journal of Phenomenological Psychology;* André Godin (b. 1915), director of the Belgian Center for Religious Education and chief editor of *Lumen Vitae,* a periodical publishing studies in the psychology of religion; and Joseph Donceel (b. 1906), professor at Fordham University. Donceel has published a textbook in philosophical psychology which has appeared in three editions, the latest of which is entitled *Philosophical Anthropology* (1967). An influential and successful text, a product of close contact with both American and European thought, this book interprets the European phenomenological viewpoints for its readers thoroughly and clearly.

THEORETICAL CONTRIBUTIONS

The natural sciences are conditioned by discoveries and accumulation of new facts about the material universe by the collective efforts of many scientists. The history of philosophy is conditioned, however, by gifted individuals whose new insights and doctrines are original enough to challenge the entrenched views and powerful enough to win the support and following of thoughtful people. The two individuals introduced here belong to such a class of philosophers.

Widely separated by age (almost 20 years), national origin, intellectual background, and research interests—one a biologist, the other originally a child and educational psychologist—these two highly ranked philosophers eventually met on the same philosophical path, interacting and borrowing ideas from each other. When Buytendijk, the biologist, came to philosophical reflection from the demands of his biological studies, he found a congenial philosophy which met his intellectual needs in Merleau-Ponty, the psychologist-later-turned-philosopher. Conversely, Merleau-Ponty discovered probings and ideas in Buytendijk which agreed well with his own pursuits. Through their continuous absorbing search for answers, and through the originality of their thought and accomplishments, they became powerful catalysts for philosophers and psychologists, leading them to the exploration of new areas of the phenomenological domain.

F. J. J. Buytendijk

Buytendijk was born in Holland in 1887. Although he obtained a medical degree in 1910, he did not practice medicine; instead he chose an academic career. University appointments took him to Amsterdam, Groningen, Nijmegen, and Utrecht. At Groningen he was professor of physiology and director of the Physiological Institute. Until he was almost 50 years old, his research was exclusively in physiology, zoology, and comparative psychology. Gradually he turned to psychology and philosophy, but without abandoning his biological springboard. Profoundly impressed by the French existential philosophy, he directed his attention to phenomenological and existential problems. Most of his works were published in Dutch, but many were translated into other languages. His work *Pain* (first Dutch publication, 1943), which was dedicated to Michotte "in token of friendship," has been available in English since 1962. In 1957 a commemorative collection of articles in phenomenological psychology and psychopathology was published in Buytendijk's honor on his 70th birthday, under the title *Rencontre/Encounter/Begegnung: Contributions toward a Human Psychology*. The bibliography of Buytendijk, included in this publication, contains 245 items.

After several years of research on the physiological basis of animal and human behavior, Buytendijk found the physiological account of man inadequate. As he stated, "Behavior can never be reduced to physiological processes and explained as a result of the integration of reflexes." He did not dismiss the physiological approach but sought to integrate it with the phenomenological study of man. Buytendijk maintained that psychology must focus its attention on man as a being existing in the world. In his opinion we are indebted to Husserl for the development of psychology as "a science of the human being and of the world of man." His phenomenological studies included research on the posture and motion of man, the psychology of women, artistic expressions, pain, touch, feelings, and emotions, as well as on dance and sports. His book *Woman* (in Dutch, 1958; English translation, 1968) is a remarkable example of a sophisticated phenomenological study of woman's biological nature, appearance, and mode of existence (being-in-the-world). Out of Buytendijk's studies of human relations came the concept of *encounter,* which has become a popular and much discussed term in phenomenological literature. Basically, encounter refers to a meeting, relation, or a meaningful communication between people which can express itself in various forms, more or less intimate, and at different levels. The term encounter is now popular in America, and the encounter movement, which will be discussed later, has grown, but the interpretation and application of that encounter idea differ sharply from those of the Dutch psychologist.

If it is true that "nowhere else than in the Netherlands has the phenomenological method been used so expertly and with such an ingenious originality for the renewal of psychology and psychiatry," as W. A. Luijpen said in his *Existential Phenomenology* (1960), Buytendijk has had an essential part in it. Versatile in both German and French in addition to his native Dutch, he has maintained an intimate contact with phenomenological and existential literature, as well as establishing personal relations with its representatives. Among the French phenomenologists to whom Buytendijk felt a particular affinity and to whose popularity in the Netherlands he contributed was Merleau-Ponty.

Maurice Merleau-Ponty

Even in his thirties, Maurice Merleau-Ponty (1908-1961) was widely acclaimed as one of the ablest philosophers of contemporary France. His philosophy was regarded as the most original and most successful integration of phenomenology and psychology. Much was expected from him, but his premature death at 53 abruptly terminated his brilliant career.

Merleau-Ponty was born in Rocheford-sur-Mer, on the west coast of France. A succession of university appointments attests to his recognition: professorship of philosophy first at the University of Lyon, then at the Sorbonne, and finally the chair at the Collège de France, the most distinguished position for a philosopher in France. For a time he was closely associated with Jean-Paul Sartre as friend, co-founder, and co-editor of *Les Temps Modernes,* a notable existential magazine. Philosophical and political differences which gradually arose between the two led to their estrangement. Merleau-Ponty was very impressed by Husserl, especially by the last phase of Husserl's thought, then still buried in unpublished manuscripts which he studied in the Husserl Archives in Louvain.

Remy C. Kwant in *The Phenomenological Philosophy of Merleau-Ponty* states, "One who wants to make a philosophical study of our world can hardly avoid a confrontation with Merleau-Ponty's thought. . . . His eyes are wide open to the fundamental facts of our period and he is full of the spirit of our era. His philosophy most strikingly mirrors both the light and the shadows of our time." Merleau-Ponty also had a knowledge of modern psychology and an appreciation of its problems. Even though his commitment was to philosophy and his discussions of psychological matters served him only as a stepping stone in his philosophical discourse, there is much relevance and thought-provoking material for psychologists in his writings. Of special interest to psychologists are his two major works: *Structure du comportement* (completed, 1938; published, 1942; 2nd ed., 1949; translated into English as *The Structure of Behavior,* 1963) and *La Phénoménologie de la perception* (1945; translated into English as *Phenomenology of Perception,* 1962). Both have been widely discussed both here and abroad. Interest in Merleau-Ponty's philosophy and its influence have steadily grown among American psychologists.

It is probably Merleau-Ponty's writings more than any other phenomenological works which not only gained sympathy and support for phenomenology in America but also supplied the most intelligible and attractive philosophical framework for those already convinced of the value and usefulness of the phenomenological approach. One of the reasons for Merleau-Ponty's appeal was his familiarity with psychological schools, various experimental findings, and also neurology and psychopathology. He made copious references to these fields and used them to illustrate some of his arguments. The main targets of his criticism of modern psychology were atomism, introspectionism, and reductionism.

In the first sentence of *The Structure of Behavior,* Merleau-Ponty expressed the aim and program of his inquiry: "to understand the relations between consciousness and nature." Through "nature," he understood all external events in their causal relationship. There is a fundamental difference between nature and consciousness, because the latter is not subject to causality. He reached this conclusion after studying various forms of behavior, including consciousness, which he approached from the behavioristic viewpoint—that is, also as a specific form of behavior. Behavior is always structured and, he held, the methods used in psychology, are inadequate to study it as behavior. The appropriate method for studying behavior is, instead, systematic phenomenology of perception. Human behavior consists of three levels: the physical, the vital (biological), and the human (psychic). Each possesses its own dynamic form. The highest and most specifically human is the third level, which, however, is dependent in its emergence on the integration of the two lower levels. Maintaining that mind is neither reducible to physical reality nor entirely cut off from it, Merleau-Ponty avoids the extremes of both the Lockean and the Cartesian conceptions of man's mental life.

In *Phenomenology of Perception,* Merleau-Ponty's main purpose was not the systematic analysis of perception for its own sake, but the derivation of a firm basis from it for his philosophical synthesis. Why did he choose perception as a foundation of his philosophy? Merleau-Ponty wanted to understand the essential feature of man, which is, in his opinion, the dialectic—that is, the dynamic relationship and inter-change—between consciousness and reality. This dialectic is achieved and reflected in the perceptual process. To him, perception is man's primordial contact with the world: "It opens a window onto things," and as such it should be a starting point for the study of man and the world.

The sequence of topics in *Phenomenology of Perception* reflects the author's course of reasoning to achieve his aim. After a succinct exposition of his view on phenomenology whose task, as he put it, is to "reveal the mystery of the world and of reason," he proceeds first to remove "traditional prejudices" which stand in the way of fruitful phenomenological exploration. These prejudices are the elementistic and associationist views of consciousness. The next task is to explore man's phenomenal field. The first component of this exploration is focused on the body or bodily being, and the second component on the world as perceived by man. In the first part of the book Merleau-Ponty shows how the physiological and psychological accounts of the body are inadequate. He considers various aspects of bodily being, such as body image, body in terms of space, body as moving, body as sexual being, and, finally, body as expressing itself in gestures and speech. In these discussions he makes extensive use of psychopathology and neurology to illustrate or support his statements. The second part, dealing with perception, analyzes the sundry facets of the perceptual process. The third part, "Being-for Itself and Being-in the World" (*être-pour-soi* and *être-au-monde*), is speculative and closely related to Merleau-Ponty's main philosophical theme.

One of the concepts stressed by Merleau-Ponty is *Lebenswelt,* a concept he first found in Husserl's unpublished manuscripts. *Lebenswelt,* variously translated most frequently now as "life-world" and sometimes as "world of everyday life" or "world of lived experiences," was assimilated by other phenomenologists, as mentioned earlier. It has also received various interpretations in phenomenological-existential literature. In general, however, it refers to the world as experienced, or perceived subjectively, by an individual person. Further light on Merleau-Ponty's latest thought has been shed by posthumous publications of his manuscripts and lectures, especially by a collection of fragments of his projected book, *Le Visible et invisible* (1964; English translation, *The Visible and the Invisible,* 1968).

PHENOMENOLOGICAL PSYCHOLOGY IN EUROPE AFTER WORLD WAR II

In the period since World War II, the influence of phenomenology on various areas of psychology has steadily increased in many Western European countries. It is not possible to give even a cursory account of the expressions and gains of phenomenological psychology in Europe in a book as concise as this one. As far as we know, there has not been any historical overview of European phenomenological psychology, not even of a single country, to which we can refer our readers. Spiegelberg (1972a) did not attempt to give an account of the postwar period "country by country," even regarding Germany, with whose phenomenology he is well acquainted. He remarked that "to obtain a fair picture of the state of phenomenology in today's German psychology would be a forbidding task." Thus, the following is only a fragmentary picture of phenomenological psychology in a few European countries.

Germany

"In a sense," Spiegelberg wrote about Germany, "phenomenology seems to be everywhere and nowhere, permeating practically all textbooks, monographs, and papers. . . ." In an encyclopedic handbook of psychology, *Handbuch der Psychologie* (begun in 1960), composed of 12 volumes and still growing, the word *Phänomenologie* "is ubiquitous," said Spiegelberg. Among the older generation of contemporary German psychologists, who assimilated the phenomenological orientation and wove it into their works on various problems, have been Johannes von Allesch, Philip Lersch, Wolfgang Metzger, Karl Mierke (d. 1971), Hans Thomae, and Albert Wellek—all distinguished names in German psychology. Wellek (1904-1972) was professor of psychology and director of the Psychological Institute at the University of Mainz. While personality theory was perhaps his dominating interest, he was also intensely concerned throughout his career with the nature and methodology of psychology as a science, perceiving it in the phenomenological spirit. He defined psychology as "neither a natural science (*Naturwissenschaft*) nor a humanistic science (*Geisteswissenschaft*), but something *sui generis,* having its own specific problems and method; its subject is invariably: experience, behavior, and mental 'structure' " (1971). Wellek was thoroughly familiar with American psychology, and his liaison with the United States, which he visited six times, was close. Wellek gave us (1968) first-hand information of considerable historical value about the effect of German immigration on the development of American psychology. In his autobiography, he singled out some American psychologists who particularly impressed him: Gordon Allport, Henry Murray, David McClelland, Roman Jakobson, Robert MacLeod, and Magda Arnold, whom he called the standard-bearer of the psychology of emotions. Of himself he said that he "represented and does represent in Germany the 'third force' of the Americans, which has always been here [Germany] the first force."

Among the younger generation of contemporary German psychologists, one figure stands out: Carl F. Graumann (b. 1923), director of the Institute of Psychology at the University of Heidelberg. He was a co-editor of a series of phenomenological-psychological studies (1960) and is presently one of the editors of the German journal *Zeitschrift für Sozial-Psychologie* and the American *Journal of Phenomenological Psychology.* His interests include theory and methodology of psychology, social perception, and psycholinguistics. It is interesting to note that the area to which several phenomenologically oriented psychologists in Europe seem to gravitate is psycholinguistics, along with the phenomenology of language.

The Netherlands

As we noted before, Holland has had many able and original phenomenologists and a productive group of phenomenological psychologists. In Holland the phenomenological and existential elements are knit closely together in individual psychologists and philosophers to such a degree that categorizing them into phenomenologists and existentialists is pointless. Buytendijk is a good example of the intertwining of both philosophies and approaches. Among active phenomenological psychologists and philosophers have been Johannes J. Linschoten (1925-1964), D. J. van Lennep (b. 1896), and Stephan Strasser (b. 1905). Linschoten was director of the Psychological Laboratory at the University of Utrecht. He advocated the notion that experimental research in psychology can be exact and fruitful only if the object of this research is first subjected to phenomenological study. He illustrated this type of study in his few skillful phenomenological analyses, one of which was the phenomenology of the experience of falling asleep. His book on William James's phenomenology (1961) generated much interest in this country and was translated by A. Giorgi (1970, *On the Way Toward a Phenomenological Psychology: The Psychology of William James*).

Van Lennep is the director of the Institute of Clinical and Industrial Psychology in Utrecht. Active in the field of projective techniques, he developed a projective test, the Four Picture Test, which in its rationale, use, and interpretation was based on phenomenological principles. He also gave a sample of interesting phenomenological analyses of everyday experiences.

Stephan Strasser was born in Vienna. He first studied there and then went to the University of Dijon, France. After lecturing at the University of Louvain, he was nominated professor of philosophical anthropology at the University of Nijmegen in Holland in 1947. In 1957 he was in the United States as a visiting professor of philosophical psychology at Duquesne University. Strasser's first book to be translated here was *The Soul in Metaphysical and Empirical Psychology* (1950; English translation, 1957). In 1963 *Phenomenology and the Human Sciences* appeared, subtitled "A Contribution to a New Scientific Ideal." In this book Strasser critically reviewed the basic characteristics and tendencies of modern science and proposed a new concept of science which includes a psychology based on phenomenological principles and insights. His article *Phenomenologies and Psychologies* (1965) was a concise review of the relations between various forms of phenomenology and psychology. It helped to clarify an issue baffling the uninitiated and is often cited.

A large proportion, if not most, of the influence of European phenomenology on American psychology in the last two decades has come via Holland—through Dutch books translated into English, articles by Dutch authors in American journals, lectures by visiting scholars from Holland, and also visits of American psychologists to universities in Holland. The dissemination of the phenomenological-existential approach in America was greatly aided by a Dutch-born psychologist, Adrian van Kaam, of whom we shall speak later.

France

French phenomenologists, especially Merleau-Ponty, were keenly interested in psychology and psychological processes such as perception, memory, and emotion. Their direct influence on French psychology, however, is not immediately apparent. Reuchlin (1964), describing trends in French psychology, did not mention phenomenology as one of them. According to him, the psychoanalytic movement "constitutes undoubtedly the most apparent characteristic of the recent developments." Lapointe (1971), on the other hand, wrote that "very few thinkers in France have completely escaped the 'influence' of Sartre." Nevertheless, it appears that phenomenologists such as Merleau-Ponty had greater impact on psychology outside France than inside. French existential works are promptly translated and eagerly read. Simone de Beauvoir (b. 1908), a close follower and collaborator with Sartre, for example, continues to publish books which are of interest to psychologists. Her famous psychological study of woman and femininity, in English translation *The Second Sex* (1953), earned the esteem of psychologists such as Buytendijk. Her latest study of aging, in English translation *The Coming of Age* (1972), also deserves attention by psychologists studying the psychology of old age: it is an insightful, penetrating, and well-documented analysis of aging.

Britain

British psychology has not shown much interest in the phenomenological approach, although some of its pioneers, such as C. Spearman, had encountered phenomenology. There are signs, however, which indicate that phenomenology has found support in certain quarters. An explicit plea for the phenomenological foundation of psychology is found in N. E. Wetherick's article *Can There Be Non-Phenomenological Psychology?* (1972). The author concludes that there "can be no such thing as non-phenomenological psychology" and that only phenomenological assumptions offer hope for the future of psychology. Judging from a book such as *New Pathways in Psychology: Maslow and the Post-Freudian Revolution* by Colin Wilson (1972), it seems that the American "Third Force," and Maslow's theories in particular, may further interest in phenomenology and existentialism in Britain and in other European countries. Britain's R. D. Laing, whom we shall discuss in the chapter on existentialism, has already attracted much attention to wider issues of phenomenological and existential psychology and psychiatry.

Other Countries

Belgium, Italy, Switzerland, and other countries have psychologists with definite phenomenological leanings or clear commitment to phenomenology as a theory and method. Belgium's Georges Thines, professor of psychology at the University of Louvain, is a dedicated phenomenologist. His main interest is comparative psychology, to which he has applied the phenomenological approach. He serves as a coeditor of Duquesne's *Journal of Phenomenological Psychology*. Switzerland's Hans Kunz and Wilhelm Keller belong to the phenomenologically inclined group: their writings, dealing either with more general problems of man and his nature or with specific psychological processes and activities, are based on a phenomenological standpoint. If any psychologist in Italy could be labeled phenomenological, it is Agostino Gemelli (1878–1959), a pupil of Külpe. Gemelli was not only familiar with but was greatly impressed by the works of Buytendijk, David Katz, and Michotte. He and his collaborators conducted numerous ingenious studies in perception, movement, feeling, and language which bore the trademark of experimental phenomenology.

It is not possible to yet determine whether phenomenology has entered the psychology of Communist countries on a large scale. For a long time, phenomenology and Marxism seemed incompatible, and the two philosophies ignored and dismissed each other. Eventually, however, a dialogue between the two developed, resulting in works by Western and Eastern European authors which try to show the convergence and complementarity of the two doctrines. This kind of thinking is exemplified in the work of a prominent Italian phenomenologist, Enzo Paci (b. 1911), whose book has been translated into English (*The Function of the Sciences and the Meaning of Man,* 1972). In this book the author devoted considerable attention to psychology and its scientific character. In view of this rapprochement between phenomenology and Marxism, one may expect that psychologists in Eastern Europe may now be better disposed toward phenomenological psychology, particularly in countries where phenomenology was well represented before World War II. A case in question may be Poland, where the phenomenologically oriented Kazimierz Twardowski (1866–1938), Brentano's student, created the most influential philosophical school in that country. During his 35-year academic career he educated generations of psychologists and philosophers, who later represented his thought at every Polish university.

Appraisal

The brief account above omitted psychotherapists and psychopathologists. They are considered in the chapter on existentialism because of the preponderance of the existential strain in the views and practices of this group of clinicians. Phenomenological psychology in Europe, generally, is strongly entrenched, widely represented, and in certain areas such as personality, perception, and psychotherapy, highly productive. German psychology, understandably, has shown the closest and most consistent allegiance to phenomenology. Metzger (1965) described German psychology of the 1960s as characterized by a tendency toward phenomenology, by a deeply ingrained distrust of purely empiricist views, and by a disdain for elementism and excessive objectivism. But phenomenological psychology has never, in Germany or in other countries, been monolithic in theory and practice. It manifests wide differences in conceptualizations, interests, and philosophical commitment. Its ties with phenomenological philosophy and other psychological doctrines are close: Brentano, Dilthey, Husserl, Scheler, and Gestalt theory have cast a long and enduring shadow on European psychology. Spiegelberg (1972a), as a professional phenomenological philosopher and a historian of the phenomenological movement, examined the phenomenological ancestry and the validity of phenomenological claims in European, especially German, psychology and psychiatry. He also weighed the positive and negative effects of the phenomenological influence on these two fields. The final balance, according to him, is favorable for phenomenology. He cautioned, however, that phenomenological psychology has its limitations, and that its function is not to replace scientific psychology, but "to aid it by enriching and strengthening it in its foundations as well as in its powers of understanding and guiding."

It must be noted, nonetheless, that phenomenological psychology in Europe has encountered a real rival and challenger in behavioristic psychology, especially the Skinnerian brand, an American import which has been steadily gaining strength on the European psychological market. On the other hand, the American "Third Force," the humanistic movement, and especially the more palpable and easily definable Maslowian psychology seem to be making an impression on Europeans and finding support. They may, in turn, reinforce the existing phenomenological orientation and raise the value of the domestic product. The characterization of European phenomenological psychology, as briefly sketched above, should be contrasted with the American phenomenological psychology when we discuss it in the next chapter. But before we review the American scene, let us specify and give a synopsis of the main features of phenomenological psychology as manifested during its long history.

CHARACTERISTICS OF PHENOMENOLOGICAL PSYCHOLOGY

There have been different conceptions and misconceptions of phenomenological psychology. In the *broadest* sense, any psychology which considers personal experience in its subject matter, and which accepts and uses phenomenological description, explicitly or implicitly, can be called phenomenological psychology. It is contrasted with psychology which admits only objective observation of behavior and excludes introspection and phenomenological description in its methodology. This broad definition of phenomenological psychology is the one most widely held and was implicit in the writings of historian E. G. Boring.

In the *strictest* sense, phenomenological psychology is the Husserlian psychology which stands apart from empirical psychology and serves as a stepping stone to a more radical form of phenomenology, transcendental phenomenology. In between is the concept of psychology which (1) follows Husserl's motto of "going to the things themselves" ("*zu den Sachen selbst*")—that is, letting the thing itself show itself in consciousness; (2) bases its philosophical justification on phenomenological philosophy, broadly conceived as the study of the data of consciousness as immediately given, whose validity is founded on the notion of intentionality but otherwise remains unfettered by any particular system of phenomenological philosophy; (3) consistently applies the phenomenological method, that is, unbiased description of phenomena; and (4) faithfully explores human experience in all its facets without philosophical preconceptions. In this understanding, phenomenological psychology is not a school or a theoretical system similar to associationism, Gestalt psychology, or psychoanalysis. It is a viewpoint, an approach, an orientation, and a methodology in psychological explorations.

Vital to phenomenological psychology is the assumption that, as Joseph F. Donceel (1967) put it, "all scientific observations and theories are ultimately based on the direct, immediate, spontaneous experience of everyday life, which phenomenology uncovers." The same tenet was formulated by Merleau-Ponty in these words: "The whole universe of science is built upon the world as directly experienced, and if we want to subject science itself to rigorous scrutiny and arrive at a precise assessment of its meaning and scope, we must begin by reawakening the basic experience of the world of which science is the second-order expression."

The following characteristics further indicate the nature of phenomenological psychology and its relationship to other trends in psychology:

1. Its basic *method* is the phenomenological method as described before. Additional methods and techniques appropriate for the study of man's experience and relation to himself, to others, and to the world are continually sought and developed.
2. Its *goal* is understanding man in all his aspects.
3. Its primary *interest* lies in human experience and its qualitative exploration. It also studies behavior but is opposed to the exclusive restriction of the subject matter of psychology to behavior and its control.
4. It rejects any philosophical assumptions concerning the nature of consciousness, except its intentionality. It particularly opposes the empiricists' *tabula rasa* concept of consciousness, the associationist view, and all reductionist tendencies.
5. It favors and stresses the holistic approach to the study of psychological problems.

The above characteristics are not evident in the thinking of all phenomenological psychologists, and if any of these characteristics are evident, they may not manifest themselves in every phenomenological psychologist to the same degree. These characteristics do tend to underlie, at least implicitly, their views and investigations, however. The phenomenological approach, now often blended with the existential orientation, has been applied to various, if not all, areas of psychology—theoretical, experimental, and clinical. Phenomenological psychologists insist that their psychology is not a closed system but is an ever-growing and expanding movement, in continuous dialectic with other orientations.

SUMMARY

We reviewed the phenomenological tradition, which did exist in psychology before Husserl, and the phenomenological trend in psychology after Husserl. Major representatives of phenomenological psychology in Europe and their contributions, both experimental and theoretical, were enumerated. The variability of phenomenological psychology in its foundation and practice was exemplified. A description of the main characteristics of phenomenological psychology concluded the chapter

Phenomenological Psychology:

Definition: An approach or orientation in psychology consisting of unbiased exploration of consciousness and experience. The phenomena are intuited, analyzed, and described as they appear in consciousness without any preconceptions. The intention of phenomenological psychology is not to replace other psychological movements and orientations, but to complement them.

Early practice: Goethe (1810), Purkinje (between 1819-1825), Hering (1834-1918).

Phenomenology as propaedeutics to psychology: Carl Stumpf (1848-1936).

Experimental phenomenology: Göttingen and Würzburg Schools, David Katz (1884-1953), Gestalt School, Albert E. Michotte (1881-1965).

Theoretical orientation: Maurice Merleau-Ponty (1908-1961), F. J. J. Buytendijk (b. 1887).

SUGGESTED READINGS

The most helpful historical account is:

Spiegelberg, H. *Phenomenology in psychology and psychiatry: A historical introduction.* Evanston: Northwestern University Press, 1972.

Theoretical issues are discussed in:

Giorgi, A. *Psychology as a human science: A phenomenologically based approach.* New York: Harper & Row, 1970.
Wann, T. W. (Ed.) *Behaviorism and phenomenology:Contrasting bases for modern psychology.* Chicago: University of Chicago Press, 1964.
Articles by R. B. MacLeod (1947, 1954, 1970a, and 1970b),

articles and books by S. Strasser (1957-58, 1963, 1965, and 1969), articles by A. Wellek (1957 and 1972), and an article by H. Winthrop (1963). Bibliographical details of these publications will be found in the general bibliography at the end of the book.

3

Phenomenological Psychology in America

During the first three decades of the twentieth century, American psychologists were scarcely aware of Husserl's philosophy and the phenomenological movement. Neither the intellectual climate nor the course of events in American psychology was conducive to giving phenomenology an impartial hearing. American psychology was moving away from German psychology and developing its own functional character. Titchener, always abreast of developments in Germany, knew of Husserl and had read him, it will be remembered, but he did not find in Husserl anything useful for psychology in his understanding of the word. When behaviorism appeared on the scene, rejection of introspection, emphasis on objective methods, quantification, rigorous experimentation, and abandonment of consciousness as the subject of psychology became the dominant trends—trends difficult to reconcile with the phenomenological approach. A factor particularly antagonistic to phenomenology was the intentional and radical dissociation of American psychology from philosophy. In Europe, where psychology kept close quarters with philosophy and was resistant to the behavioristic trend, phenomenology had a better chance to exert its influence on psychological thought, as it indeed did. It was not until the 1920s and 1930s, when the Gestaltist studies found favorable reception in America, that the phenomenological method as practiced by the Gestalt psychologists met with a more sympathetic reaction. Still, few American psychologists were willing to undertake phenomenological research and not much attention was paid to such research being conducted in Europe. However, after World War II, European phenomenological thought began to attract more attention.

William James: First American Phenomenologist?

There is no solid evidence that William James was familiar with Husserl's philosophy. He knew Stumpf, with whom he maintained close and friendly relations, and he was acquainted with Stumpf's concept of phenomenology, on which he commented favorably. Husserl, on the other hand, not only knew James's psychology but was impressed with it and acknowledged his debt to James more than once. However, can James be called a phenomenologist? Several authors considered this question and some researched this problem thoroughly. Spiegelberg (1972a), noting that the term "phenomenology" never occurs in James's writings and that the new American phenomenological psychologists do not refer to James in their works, credited "the spirit of James's bold and open-minded psychology" with creating "a climate in which phenomenology could take root among American psychologists." Some writers went further and thought that if James's "stream of consciousness" and other ideas concerning consciousness (what Wilshire (1968) called James's "protophenomenology") had been developed and followed seriously, America might have had its own brand of phenomenological psychology. According to Linschoten (1970) and Wilshire (1968), James anticipated modern phenomenology, occasionally practiced phenomenological analysis, and pointed out the advantages of the phenomenological approach as well as the dangerous consequences of its rejection. James's psychology and his own brand of phenomenology are called "noteworthy and timely" (Wilshire, 1968) even today and are more understandable because they are presented in clear language which ordinary people can understand (MacLeod, 1969).

THE IMMIGRATION OF EUROPEAN
PHENOMENOLOGISTS

Among the factors which were critical in arousing America's interest in phenomenology and contributing to its being more widely and better known were increased intellectual communication between Europe and America, more frequent personal contacts between psychologists of various countries, the translation of major phenomenological works into English, and, most significantly, the immigration of European, especially German, psychologists to the United States because of Nazi persecution. There were many German and Austrian psychologists, acquainted with and sympathetic to phenomenological thought, who made America their home. In addition to the well-known Gestalt psychologists such as, first, the famous trio of Koffka, Köhler, and Wertheimer, and Solomon Asch, Karl Duncker, and Kurt Lewin, the German and Austrian psychologists included eminent scholars such as Rudolf Allers, Magda Arnold, Charlotte and Karl Bühler, Albin Gilbert, Hans Hahn, Fritz Heider, Martin Scheerer, Wilhelm Stern, and Heinz Werner. Some of these psychologists are mentioned later. Moreover, several prominent German scientists and philosophers associated with European phenomenology and with already-established reputations settled in America, where they significantly enhanced the phenomenological movement through their writings, academic positions, and other activities. Some examples are Erwin W. Straus, a psychiatrist; Aron Gurwitsch, a philosopher; and Kurt Goldstein, a psychopathologist and psychologist.

Kurt Goldstein

Among the scientists who immigrated to the United States were individuals who, although neither calling themselves phenomenologists nor giving evidence of being directly influenced by phenomenology, expressed views and conducted research compatible with and even strikingly parallel to the phenomenological viewpoint. One such scientist was Kurt Goldstein (1878-1965), whose views on emotions, the theory of the organism, his holistic viewpoint, and other aspects of his work were in close agreement with phenomenology. Phenomenologists listened to Goldstein and viewed his work and opinions with respect and approval.

Goldstein researched in the fields of anatomy, physiology, neurology, psychology, and psychiatry and published over 300 articles and books. He began his career in medicine and received his medical degree in 1903. After a decade of delving into psychopathology and nervous disorders, he was made director of a Frankfurt institute for brain-injured soldiers. His work at the institute dealt largely with the effects of brain injury on sensory and motor functions, perception, tonus, and language. The studies which came from his work caused Goldstein to reconsider the concept of cerebral localization and the dynamics of higher mental functioning. He became convinced that man's functioning or malfunctioning could not be understood in part-whole terms but must be viewed in holistic terms. *The Organism* (1933), which was undoubtedly Goldstein's most significant publication, presented his theory of the unitary or holistic functioning of all nervous events, challenging the predominant theory of the time.

Goldstein came to America in 1935. He continued to publish, in addition to teaching and conducting a private practice. With the English translation of *The Organism,* subtitled *A Holistic Approach to Biology Derived from Pathological Data in Man* (1939), Goldstein had a second career in which his theory was applied to areas of personality and cognition. The significance of his contributions was not so much that they formed a specific or limited doctrine, though that existed, but that they engendered an enthusiasm for investigation and discourse as well as encouraging the ability to consolidate diversified fields. Goldstein eventually came to exert a wide influence on American neurological, psychiatric, biological, and psychological thought, but, more importantly, he became a living presence among thinkers interested in the ultimate structural and functional questions of man and his environment. A collection of 20 essays, *The Reach of Mind* (Simmel, 1968), has been published in memory of Kurt Goldstein and includes articles by Erich Fromm, Gardner Murphy, Rollo May, and 15 other prominent individuals.

Erwin W. Straus

In the late 1920s, a new direction in European psychopathology emerged, called the anthropological. It was represented by Ludwig Binswanger, Viktor von Gebsattel, the young Erwin Straus, and by their journal, *Der Nervenarzt* (*The Neurologist*), founded in 1930. Active as a psychiatrist and author in Europe, Straus (b. 1891) was drawn more deeply into phenomenology only after his arrival in the United States in 1939. After a professorship of psychology at Black Mountain College in North Carolina until 1944, and then a two-year research fellowship at Johns Hopkins University, he joined the Veterans Administration Hospital staff in Lexington, Kentucky in 1946. During his tenure at this institution, he has become an effective promoter of phenomenology in psychology and psychiatry. Thanks to his efforts, international conferences entitled "Phenomenology Pure and Applied" have been organized and convened in Lexington since 1963, attended by philosophers as well as by psychiatrists and psychologists. His book, published first in Germany in 1935, was translated from the second German edition into English in 1963 as *The Primary World of Senses: A Vindication.* It treats a wide spectrum of perceptual problems from a phenomenological point of view. A collection of 18 of his papers, some available in English for the first time, and his preface comprise another book, *Phenomenological Psychology* (1966), dealing with a variety of theoretical, experimental, and clinical questions. In the author's own evaluation of the book, the leitmotif of all the papers was "to decipher the unwritten constitution of everyday life." The title for this volume was chosen, he wrote, "to express an affiliation with the phenomeno-logical movement." Although Straus did not follow Husserl on his path to transcendental reduction, he complied with Husserl's appeal, "Back to the things themselves," by attempting to reveal the depth and wealth of human experience instead of reducing it.

Straus's major role in phenomenology in America was that of a catalyst by keeping the phenomenological cause alive, inviting others to support it, and stimulating and teaching those who were in the orbit of his influence. A *Festschrift* in commemoration of his 75th birthday, entitled *Conditio Humana* (1966), attested to this influence.

Aron Gurwitsch

After studying under Stumpf, Husserl, and Goldstein, Aron Gurwitsch (b. 1901) went to Frankfurt, where he became acquainted with Gestalt psychology and wrote his doctoral dissertation on the relation between Gestalt psychology and phenomenology. He spent six years in France, where he met Gabriel Marcel and Merleau-Ponty. After his immigration to the United States in 1939, he held various academic positions before he was appointed professor of philosophy at the New School of Social Research in New York City in 1959. His writings display familiarity with contemporary psychological thought and concern with the philosophical basis of psychological science. He devoted special attention to the field of consciousness in articles and a book, *The Field of Consciousness,* first published in French in 1957 and then in English in 1964. This book has been praised as a distinguished work in phenomenological psychology. A collection of his articles published from 1929 to 1961 appeared in 1966, called *Studies in Phenomenology and Psychology.* In his academic position, Gurwitsch trained a group of phenomenologists who later distinguished themselves in various fields of philosophy and psychology. A number of his students who obtained their Ph.D. degrees under his mentorship now teach at various American universities.

The Role of Ernst Cassirer

As we trace the intellectual genealogy of European-born scholars who immigrated to America and helped develop American psychology, we cannot overlook the German philosopher Ernst Cassirer (1874-

1945). A former professor at Hamburg University, Cassirer arrived in the United States late in his life, in 1941, and taught at Yale and Columbia universities. While in America he published *An Essay on Man* (1944), but his major work was *Philosophie der symbolischen Formen* in three volumes (1923-1929; in English, *The Philosophy of Symbolic Forms,* 1953). His philosophy, born from the neo-Kantian approach, left a mark which was clearly evident and explicitly acknowledged on several American scientists and philosophers of European origin. When one considers Cassirer's friendly relations with Husserl and phenomenology, one can understand the sympathetic attitude toward phenomenology in his former students and in those who had intellectual ties with him. Among those who later often gave testimony to their indebtedness to Cassirer and cited his ideas were his cousin Kurt Goldstein, his colleague Wilhelm Stern, and Stern's students and co-workers at the University of Hamburg, Fritz Heider, Martin Scheerer, and Heinz Werner.

Cassirer's importance and his extensive influence stem from his highly original work on symbolic activity in man and human life. He urged that man be defined as *animal symbolicum,* since man's symbolic activity is the most characteristic feature of human existence which sets man apart from animals and provides the foundation for the whole development of culture. Symbolism and symbolic activities, largely ignored by psychology in the past, have recently become topics of vivid interest and study for humanistically oriented psychologists.

BEGINNINGS AND PROGRESS

We shall now consider the circumstances of phenomenology's appearance on the American psychological scene, as well as the psychologists who contributed most to the infiltration and progress of the phenomenological viewpoint. There has not yet been enough basic historical research on the sources of phenomenological influences, the relations between masters and disciples, the intellectual dependence of various psychologists, the appraisal of phenomenological contributions and their effect on academic psychology, and other aspects, to allow an accurate and complete picture of the history of phenomenological psychology in the United States to be drawn. We therefore ask the reader's indulgence for the inevitable gaps and fragmentariness of our account.

Sources of Phenomenology

One should expect that American psychologists who studied in Germany or visited it after 1900 would have become aware of and perhaps affected by phenomenology. This should be particularly true in Göttingen, where Husserl lectured from 1901 to 1916, and in Munich, where students of psychology and pupils of Theodore Lipps (1851-1914), professor of psychology at the University of Munich, organized an active club known as the Munich Phenomenological Circle to discuss Husserl's phenomenology. Max Scheler was the leading figure there between 1906 and 1910. The number of American students, however, was small. One American who studied in Germany after 1900 and who indeed showed phenomenological orientation in his early work was Thomas V. Moore (1877-1969), a psychologist and later a psychiatrist as well and a pupil of both Wundt and Külpe. Moore must have known of Husserl and of psychologists' interest in him when he studied in Leipzig in 1904 and 1905, and especially when he was in Munich in 1913 and 1914. That was during the time of the Munich Phenomenological Circle, composed of many psychologists, and while Lipps, Külpe's students, and Karl and Charlotte Bühler were there. Moore can be considered one of the earliest Americans practicing experimental phenomenology because of his experimentation with abstraction and imagery (1910-1919), his support of the "imageless thought" notion, and, later, his investigation on willing and voluntary action (1922). Moore did not pursue his phenomenological and experimental interests, due to his immersion in clinical and psychiatric work, as well as to other circumstances in his personal life.

After World War I, American students traveled to Germany again, to be introduced to psychological currents of the day—Gestalt psychology, phenomenology, German typology, and psychologists such as Wilhelm Stern, Wolfgang Köhler, and Spranger, Dilthey's student. Gordon Allport (1967), who spent two years in Europe (1922-1924), acknowledged "the powerful impact" of his German teachers, an impact which was to have a lasting effect on his career and his relation to phenomenology. He supported phenomenology, and 40 years after his studies in Germany, when asked by Richard I. Evans (1971) about his view on phenomenology, he answered that he was not "immediately worried about being too phenomenological" because psychologists for so long had neglected subjective reports. Robert MacLeod's studies in Germany (1928-1929) introduced him to phenomenology and also left a mark on his thinking, which he confirmed 42 years later in an article (1970). MacLeod brought back a respect for phenomenology which he subsequently and consistently defended, earning for himself the nickname "America's Mr. Phenomenology" (Krech, 1970).

The fruits of these intellectual encounters and their effects on American psychology did not become apparent until much later, as students returning from abroad in the 1920s found psychology in this country positivistic, behavioristic, aphilosophical, antimentalistic, and anti-introspectionistic, and thus resistant and hostile to such a philosophical and mentalistic orientation as phenomenology. Better circumstances for this philosophy arose in the late 1930s when, as we have already pointed out, German philosophers and psychologists who came to America began to interpret phenomenology, Gestalt psychology, and other European movements. Referring to his meeting with these prominent refugees in New York City, Abraham Maslow (Goble, 1970) called it "the most profound learning experience" of his life. He wrote, "I think it's fair to say that I have had the best teachers, both formal and informal, of any person who ever lived, just because of the historical accident of being in New York City when the very cream of European intellect was migrating away from Hitler. New York City in those days was simply fantastic. There has been nothing like it since Athens." The full impact of this "cream of European intellect" became evident and was felt only when their research and literary productivity and their views and teachings reached wider ranks of American psychology.

In conclusion, phenomenology became known to American psychologists from these three significant sources: (1) European-born and -trained emigré phenomenologists; (2) native Americans who studied in Europe and who became the interpreters and supporters of phenomenology; and (3) translations of classical and new European phenomenological works as well as American publications on phenomenology and its meaning for psychology. But there was still another source contributing to an increased awareness of the phenomenological approach: a home-grown phenomenological orientation, derived not from philosophy or from direct contact with European phenomenologists, but coming from an American psychologist, Donald Snygg. He and his collaborator, Arthur W. Combs, who had been associated with Carl Rogers, introduced a phenomenological approach and program into a systematic psychology of behavior.

"Grassroots Phenomenology"

Donald Snygg (1904-1967), in a 1941 article entitled "The Need for a Phenomenological System of Psychology" in the *Psychological Review,* called for a psychology developed from the phenomenological viewpoint. This was the first time in an American psychological journal that someone had pleaded for a phenomenological approach to psychology. Without any reference to philosophical phenomenology, Snygg postulated that "behavior is completely determined by and pertinent to the phenomenological field of the behaving organism." Only a psychology developed along phenomenological lines could accurately predict individual behavior, he declared. Eight years later he and Arthur W. Combs (b. 1912) presented such a psychology in the book *Individual Behavior: A New Frame of Reference for Psychology*—the first such venture in American psychological literature which was later characterized by Spiegelberg (1967) as the "American phenomenology from the grassroots."

A revised edition of the book appeared in 1959 with a new subtitle, *A Perceptual Approach to Behavior*. While recognizing the contributions of objective psychology, which studies behavior from "the outside," the authors found such an approach inadequate for the study of individual behavior. They developed their system of psychology on the assumption that the key to understanding and predicting individual behavior is the world within the individual himself or within his phenomenal field. The term *phenomenal field* is used in the book synonymously with *perceptual field,* that is, "the entire universe, including himself, as it is experienced by the individual at the instant of action."

Part of the phenomenal field, and its most permanent part, is the phenomenal self or the perceived self. The phenomenal self is discussed in various aspects, such as its origin, development, characteristics, relation to the environment, and role in behavior. The basic need of human beings is to maintain and enhance the phenomenal self. The perceptual frame of reference is applied throughout the book to all basic problems of psychology, such as learning, emotion, and personality, as well as to sociology, education, and clinical situations.

The Phenomenological Problem

The increased attention to the phenomenological approach by American psychologists was reflected in the re-publication in 1959 of 14 articles which had appeared in 10 different American journals during the years 1939 through 1957. Each article dealt with matters such as the self and social psychology, presented from a viewpoint sympathetic to and compatible with the phenomenological approach. The articles appeared in a book entitled *The Phenomenological Problem* (1959). As Alfred E. Kuenzli, the editor of the book, explained, its purpose was to clarify the meaning of the phenomenological emphasis in modern psychology. The authors included Hadley Cantril, Arthur Combs and Donald Snygg, Lawrence K. Frank, Abraham S. Luchins, Theodore M. Newcomb, Victor Raimy, Carl Rogers, Saul Rosenzweig, Richard Jessor, and Robert MacLeod.

Robert B. MacLeod

Among American psychologists, Robert B. MacLeod (1907-1972) showed an early interest in psychological phenomenology and consistently pointed to its methodological values. He became familiar with German phenomenology during his studies in Frankfurt and Berlin. He met David Katz personally and, with C. W. Fox, translated Katz's book, *The World of Colour*. His article on the phenomenological approach in social psychology, published in the *Psychological Review* in 1947, elicited favorable comments here and abroad. In this article MacLeod described the phenomenological approach and outlined its potential contributions to social psychology. MacLeod's position on phenomenology both as theory and method was never extreme: in the article he stated that phenomenology is not to be a substitute for psychophysics and psychophysiology. Sixteen years later, at the symposium on behaviorism and phenomenology in 1963, he reiterated his moderate position when he spoke of phenomenology as not an exclusive approach, but as an approach which might be more useful and appropriate in certain areas than in others, and which in general might enrich psychology. He specified the experimental areas in which this approach may prove particularly fruitful. He also expressed the belief that "what in the old, prescientific days, we used to call 'consciousness' still can and should be studied." But is such a study scientific? The concept of science and what is not science underwent a considerable revision in the present century. In MacLeod's formulation, to be a scientist "is to have boundless curiosity tempered by discipline." And, as he said on another occasion (1970a), he did not really care whether psychology "is listed as a science as long as it contributes to the understanding of human behavior and human experience."

MacLeod's view that phenomenology is one of the acceptable and useful approaches in psychology and is reconcilable with other trends, including the behavioristic, is in marked contrast to some extreme opinions both for and against phenomenology. At the First Banff Conference on Theoretical Psychology, in 1965, MacLeod discussed psychological phenomenology as "a useful propaedeutic to a science of psychology" which "serves to define problems and to point the way to possible answers." In one of his latest and most thought-provoking articles, "Newtonian and Darwinian Conceptions of Man and Some Alternatives" (1970a), he called phenomenology "a fundamental challenge to the traditional scientific conception of man and his relation to the world." He succinctly described the difference between the traditional scientific approach and the phenomenological in these words:

The traditional scientist begins with the assumption of a world, of which man is a part. . . . The phenomenologist begins with experience (*Erlebnis*), of which the world is a part. . . . [He] does not deny the existence of an "outside" world, which can be described in the language of physics; he insists, however, that this is at best a partial picture, that the world we regard as "real" is an extrapolation from the world we actually experience (the phenomenal world, the *Lebenswelt*), that the very concept of "reality," which is derived from experience, must be examined as a form of experience before it can be treated as an independent existent.

Phenomenology has so far not had a better spokesman among American psychologists than MacLeod. His scholarship, open-mindedness, fairness, and modesty, together with the personal charm and engaging crisp style of his few but always interesting and provocative writings, did a great deal toward furthering phenomenological psychology in America. He was also an inspiring teacher, according to his former students, an active and always ready to serve member of the American Psychological Association. MacLeod was a man whose fine qualities won many friends for him and for the causes he sponsored.

Reactions and Attitudes Toward Phenomenology

The support which MacLeod and others gave to phenomenology ran counter to the opposition or indifference of the majority of American psychologists toward this approach from 1920 to 1950. Whatever practice or promotion of phenomenology took place during this time, it was isolated and sporadic. Only in the 1950s, and distinctly in the 1960s, did more favorable winds begin to blow for phenomenology.

The opponents of phenomenology have looked upon it as an anachronistic reversion to outdated doctrines, incompatible with the scientific character of psychology and harmful to its progress. According to some critics, phenomenology cannot be of any help, methodologically or conceptually, to a psychology "which wishes to explain and to predict on the basis of rules and manifest similarities" (Turner, 1967).

Skeptics have questioned the significance and effectiveness of phenomenological psychology in both theory and practice. They have expressed reservations about the subjectivity of phenomenological data and its validity and reliability. They have pointed to the lack or paucity of appropriate methods and techniques of investigation, over-dependence on verbal descriptions with their inherent limitations, ambiguity of phenomenological concepts, and sometimes the esoteric language of phenomenologists. These reservations or criticisms have been expressed in publications at various times and in reviews of phenomenological literature, often by authors who could not be accused of prejudice. Some phenomenological writings provoked criticism, not for their phenomenological approach, but for ignoring— in their discussions of such traditional topics in psychology as learning and memory—empirical data and contributions of unequivocal value. Berlyne (1968) thought that "in some ways" it is "a great pity that this point of view [that is, phenomenology] has not had more of a hearing in the United States, since the problems that it raises are important and worth pondering." But he doubted that a "fruitful merger" of phenomenological and behavioristic psychologies was possible and felt that in continental European countries phenomenology "has done little to speed up the development of scientific psychology." Jean Piaget (1965) likewise expressed concern about the possible detrimental effects of phenomenology on the growth of scientific psychology and warned against attempts to substitute a philosophical approach for the scientific. In *Insights and Illusions of Philosophy,* Piaget wrote, " 'Philosophical' psychology [in which he includes phenomenology] constantly criticizes scientific psychology for not ending in an 'anthropology' able to express the whole man, and I have in particular been constantly criticized for being an intellectualist because I am only interested in cognitive functions." After examining four "philosophical" psychologies—of Maine de Biran, Bergson, Sartre, and Merleau-Ponty—he concluded sardonically, "We have seen Sartre project his self into consciousness . . . to discover there that its 'causality' is magic, and we see Merleau-Ponty end by concluding that subjectivity is basically ambiguous. This is, then, what is given to us as knowledge of Man and which is opposed to the psychology of conduct, because the latter is intellectualist and only 'scientific.' "

The supporters of phenomenology have suggested that science advanced when its strongly entrenched assumptions were challenged and the searchlight of the inquiring mind was directed to the issues once pushed aside or ignored. In the same manner in psychology, MacLeod (1970a) thought, the time "may again have come for psychologists to look with a questioning eye at some of the assumptions to which we have grown accustomed." This may not usher in "a great new era," but, as he phrased it in his characteristic manner, "it is a healthy exercise, and it is fun."

Phenomenology Defended

The defenders of the phenomenological approach have pointed to the long neglect of human experience in academic psychology. As a science of man that aims toward an understanding of man, psychology has to begin with experience and its exploration. It is the exclusion of experience, phenomenology's defenders say, that has harmed psychology and limited its usefulness for human society. The theoretical or methodological deficiencies or shortcomings of the phenomenological program, whatever they may now be, cannot excuse psychologists from deliberately bypassing experience and justify their total dismissal of phenomenology. Once the phenomenological inquiry is legitimized, collective efforts may improve it, make it more effective and useful in all branches of psychology, and make its data admissible in the courts of science. Phenomenology, as Strasser (1965) expressed it, can have "a broadening, enriching, and stimulating influence" on psychology. "We need a form of psychology," May (1969a) wrote, "that does not dwell on behavior to the exclusion of experience or experience without regard for behavior, but centers on the relation between experience and behavior." That is why, it is repeatedly emphasized in phenomenological circles, phenomenology is not meant to supplant behaviorism, psychoanalysis, and other systems but to complement them. Indeed, serious attempts have been made to prove the compatibility of radical behaviorism with phenomenological (for example, Day, 1969) and existential approaches (for instance, Kvale and Grenness, 1967). The symposium of 1963 at Rice University, called "Behaviorism and Phenomenology," provided an occasion to confront the two, "contrasting bases for modern psychology." Four of its six participants suggested the possibility of coexistence of both bases. *Behaviorism and Phenomenology: Contrasting Bases for Modern Psychology,* edited by T. A. Wann, containing the papers and the discussion of this symposium, has had remarkable success and provoked a large number of articles and other responses here and abroad, attesting to the lively and wide interest in the issue.

There are psychologists in America now who go further than merely stressing the complementary role of the phenomenological approach. They are more deeply committed to the phenomenological viewpoint and see a much larger place for phenomenological psychology; they believe that the "phenomenological approach offers the best point of departure for establishing a constructive alternative to natural scientific psychology and in providing a frame of reference for conceiving psychology as a human science" (from the introduction to the first issue of the *Journal of Phenomenological Psychology,* founded in 1971).

CONTRIBUTIONS OF PHENOMENOLOGY

It is not yet possible to evaluate or measure the effect of phenomenological thought and method on American psychology. Nor is it yet possible to assess the effect of the dialogue between phenomenology and behavioristic psychology that has been going on for some time—since at least 1963. Nevertheless, even though the role of phenomenology has not been large, some developments and changes which have occurred in the last two decades can be ascribed to the direct or indirect influence of phenomenological thought and activities. This influence is reflected in some specific areas. The following observations again make no pretense of including all the inroads of phenomenology into American psychology but merely illustrate a few of the more obvious phenomenological successes in some fields.

Perception

The phenomenological method has proved to be particularly successful in the study of perception, as is widely recognized. Thanks to its skillful use by Gestaltists and others, many new perceptual phenomena were discovered and investigated. Phenomenologists introduced new concepts and theories regarding perceptual processes—for example, abandoning the sharp separation of sensation from perception —ingrained in psychology since Locke—and of perception from cognition. They stressed the dynamic and active character of perceptual activity, the intentional nature of all perceptual experience, and the idea that all perceptual experience is structural—that is, that experience exhibits many lawful regularities such as the figure-ground relation and closure.

The studies and views of James J. Gibson (b. 1904) have substantially agreed with the Gestalt-phenomenological tradition. After several years of research on visual problems and extensive experimentation on visual phenomena, Gibson published *The Perception of the Visual World* (1950), an analytical description of how man sees the world. This book dealt with a question to which all visual phenomenologists repeatedly return: the correlation of the visual field (what is exactly represented in, or impinged on, the sensory visual system—for example, the railroad tracks converging in the distance) and the visual world, that is, the objects as perceived (for example, the tracks perceived as equidistant). Gibson's description of the dependence of the visual world on the visual field contributed novel and original insights to the phenomenology of vision.

Gibson again surveyed the perceptual process in relation to sensation in *The Senses Considered as Perceptual Systems* (1966), in which he utilized information theory and proposed that the role of the senses consists of mediating and yielding information from the environment rather than supplying sensations in the traditional meaning. Referring to his own views on perception, Gibson (1967) wrote:

> The one with whom in recent years I have been in strikingly near agreement is Albert Michotte, of Louvain—in everything but the notion of external information and external meaning. . . . It is a notable lesson in the convergence of experimental science that such a man as he and such a one as I, from totally different backgrounds, should have found ourselves agreeing so thoroughly and so delightedly. . . . We got the same results. This is what counts. It makes one believe in the possibliity of getting at the truth.

An active researcher in visual perception has been Mercedes Gaffron (b. 1908). She received a Ph.D. in Berlin and an M.D. in Munich and is now associated with Duke University. Her work on Rembrandt's etchings, published in German in 1950, brought out new methods and avenues of approach in the study of esthetics. Her subsequent work in America dealt with phenomenological experiences evoked by pictures presented in systematically varied spatial orientations. These new excursions in the world of perceptual phenomena provided a basis for a critical look at the existing perceptual theories and led her to reformulate some of the fundamental issues concerning the perceptual process. Her strong emphasis has been on the scientific significance and validity of experiential properties of human perceptual activity.

Noteworthy work in this area has also been done by Karl E. Zener (b. 1903) independently and also in collaboration with Dr. Gaffron. He authored a theoretical paper on the significance for scientific psychology of experience of the individual (1958).

Personality

Phenomenologist Eduard Spranger (1882-1963), Wilhelm Dilthey's disciple, influenced the study of personality in Germany and here through his work, *Lebensformen* (1914; translated from the 6th edition, 1927, in English as *Types of Men*, 1928). His sixfold typology—theoretical, economic, esthetic, social, political, and religious types—gave inspiration to Gordon Allport (who studied under Spranger in Berlin) and Vernon for their book, *A Study of Values* (1931, rev. 1951 and 1960), and for the highly successful test now known as the Allport-Vernon-Lindzey Study of Values Test.

Theories and measures of personality based on self-concept and personal constructs have been close to phenomenology. An example is George A. Kelly (1905-1967), whose personality theory and Rep Test (Role Construct Repertory Test) was first proposed in *The Psychology of Personal Constructs* (2 vols., 1955). According to Kelly, the important determinant of a person's behavior is his own conception of the world in which he lives and of the people to whom he has or is relating. Kelly's views and clinical techniques found a considerable following and inspired a large body of empirical research and literature. A collection of 17 of Kelly's papers published by B. A. Maher (1969) showed this pioneer clinician as one who readily assimilated ideas from varied sources—phenomenology, existentialism, cognitive psychology, and behaviorism—but who wanted to see the study of the experiencing and construing person firmly rooted in the empirical, objective research of the clinic and the laboratory. "There is . . . little doubt," wrote the British psychologist Wetherick in 1972, "that psychology as we have defined it [that is, as a science whose "conceptual foundations lie in phenomenology rather than in empiricism"] will owe Kelly an immense debt and will incorporate much of his work in that part of itself concerned with personality and psychotherapy." British clinicians Bannister and Fransella, in their book *Inquiring Man: The Theory of Personal Constructs* (1971), reappraised Kelly's theory, confronted it with current issues and areas of psychology, and reviewed research stimulated by it.

Eugene T. Gendlin's (b. 1926) definition of experience, experiencing, and personal meaning, presented in his publications (1962, 1965), along with his efforts to bridge the subjective with the objective in the experiencing person, and other conceptualizations found resonance in some personality theoreticians and psychotherapists. Carl Rogers stressed the importance of Gendlin, his former student, and of Gendlin's basic theoretical framework which, Rogers acknowledged, influenced his own thought.

With regard to emotion, Magda Arnold (b. 1903) has consistently argued for the indispensability of phenomenological analysis in this field and has skillfully practiced it. In her two-volume work, *Emotion and Personality* (1960), still unsurpassed as a theoretical synthesis in the field of emotion, she used human emotional experience and its analysis as the starting point and the basis for studying the nature of emotion. "The only approach that promises a solution of the problem of how perception arouses emotion," she wrote, "is a careful phenomenological analysis of the whole sequence from perception to emotion and action."

Some other applications of the phenomenological method in the study of the person were illustrated by Mary Henle (b. 1913). In one work (1962) she showed how multiplicity in the experience of the self can be demonstrated through this method. Phenomenological analysis reveals, she wrote, that "we do not experience ourselves as a single undifferentiated 'I'; rather a number of distinguishable functions," such as actor, observer, critic, friend, dreamer, realist, and others.

At the 1960 American Psychological Association convention, a symposium was held on phenomenological conceptions of personality and was chaired by Alfred E. Kuenzli. Its papers were subsequently published in the *Journal of Individual Psychology* (1961, **17,** 4-38). The participants of the symposium were C. H. Patterson, F. P. Kilpatrick, A. Luchins, R. Jessor, and T. Landsman, the discussant. One of the symposium's purposes was to achieve better synthesis among the phenomenological psychologists. Phenomenological conceptions of personality—like other phenomenological themes—are often currently assimilated and represented by psychologists associated with the humanistic psychology movement.

Clinical Psychology

The phenomenological approach, especially the synthesis of both the phenomenological and existential elements, appealed to American clinicians, who saw in this framework a new promise for a better understanding of the patient and for a more effective psychotherapy. A sympathetic response also came from those psychologists who had independently developed similar viewpoints. The relevance of phenomenology for clinical practice was advocated first in America by Erwin Straus in the middle 1940s. Since then, the use of phenomenology together with existential thought has greatly widened in American clinical psychology and psychotherapy. While this topic is discussed in more detail in the next chapter, let us mention here a book by Joseph Lyons (b. 1918), who worked with Erwin Straus for a decade: *Psychology and the Measure of Man* (1963), with the subtitle *A Phenomenological Approach.* Lyons, who is now professor of psychology at the University of California at Davis, was well-qualified to write this book by virtue of his extensive examination of phenomenological and existential literature. In this book he attempted to, in his own words, "outline a phenomenological psychology of clinical problems." Based on European phenomenological and existential thought, this outline was addressed to American clinicians. It was not a new method or system that Lyons offered, but a re-evaluation of some basic clinical problems in the spirit of phenomenology and existentialism. The second chapter of Lyons's book was devoted to the relationship between phenomenology and psychology. In it he sets forth his phenomenological position and differentiates it from other approaches in psychology. A reviewer in *Contemporary Psychology* called the book "a significant milestone in the development of an 'authentic' psychology" and one which should be "a minor classic in contemporary psychological theorizing." Lyons's most recent formulation of psychology is to be found in his book, *Experience: An Introduction to a Personal Psychology* (1973). In it he discusses clinical issues in relation to experience and leads to a concept of personal psychology of experience.

Other Developments

Some recent developments congruent with the phenomenological viewpoint suggest that phenomenology—apart from its ostensible effects in such fields as perception, personality, psychodiagnosis, and psychotherapy—might have affected American psychology in a subtle and indirect manner. They include, for example, the wider recognition of experience as a legitimate scientific datum, the definition of psychology in some textbooks as the study of behavior *and* experience, and the extension of phenomenological analysis—although not explicitly in all cases—to a broad range of human experience and activities such as religious, esthetic, willing, suffering, and to attitudes toward death, race, institutions, and political events. The reappearance in texts of topics such as cognition, imagery, will, self, altered states of consciousness, and creativity—once considered ill-suited topics for scientific study—may also be credited, at least partly, to the influence of phenomenology. Moreover, the intense modern preoccupation with cognitive processes, man's symbolic activities, psycholinguistics, the wide appeal of Piaget's work and ideas, and developmental psychology based on the spirit of Heinz Werner may also be considered as expressions of the climatic change in American psychology which phenomenology, together with other movements, reinforced, corroborated, or helped to create.

Return of Consciousness

The reappearance of the issue of consciousness in current psychological texts and discussions may be interpreted either as a sign of wider acceptance of phenomenology or as a phenomenon of more complex origin, which has naturally helped the acceptance of phenomenology considerably. Without delving into the complexities of this phenomenon, let us simply note that there is renewed interest in consciousness as a legitimate subject of study after many decades of official silence. Consciousness has been a subject of debates between behaviorists and nonbehaviorists. Rex M. Collier said in 1964 that to him there seems "no more challenging need in psychology than to restore to our science a valid and usable concept of consciousness." It appears that the world of consciousness in its normal and altered states has been restored, being seriously discussed in current psychological literature and at meetings of psychological organizations. Still, however, there is much continued silence about consciousness; there are textbooks of general psychology which do not contain the word "consciousness" at all and which do not list it in the index.

Duquesne University

Turning to more tangible evidence of interest in phenomenology, let us call attention to the role of two universities and their presses in promoting phenomenology, to Duquesne and Northwestern Universities. Duquesne University, through its diverse and substantial contributions to phenomenological psychology, has earned the title of the capital of phenomenological psychology in the New World. This institution has been the principal center of training and research in phenomenological psychology in America for the last two decades. Its graduates now occupy academic positions in different parts of the country, where they represent and promote the phenomenological approach through teaching and research.

Duquesne has been host to prominent American and European representatives of phenomenological as well as existential psychology and philosophy, furnishing a platform for dialogue among scholars. Its University Press has published several outstanding works by American and European authors. Its international *Journal of Phenomenological Psychology,* founded in 1971, is a communication medium between phenomenological psychologists in America and other countries. The journal's policy is an expression of the present tone characterizing today's American phenomenological psychology:

> This journal is dedicated to the aim of approaching psychology in such a way that the entire range of experience and behavior of man as a human person may be properly studied. The priority is placed on the fidelity to the phenomenon of man as a whole and all aspects that are studied must be mindful of their human relatedness. The challenge facing us is to invent methods and other types of analyses that will unveil significant aspects of man's relatedness to himself, others and the world. The term

"phenomenological" is meant in the broadest sense possible, referring to the movement as a whole, and it is not intended to convey the thought of any single person.

The international character of the journal is evident in the composition of its editorial board: Amedeo Giorgi, of Duquesne University; Georges Thines, of the University of Louvain, Belgium; and Carl F. Graumann, of the University of Heidelberg, Germany.

Another product of Duquesne University is a serial edited by Amedeo Giorgi, William F. Fischer, and Rolf von Eckartsberg, all of Duquesne, called *Phenomenological Psychology*. The first volume appeared in 1971. The serial publishes theoretical articles and reports of phenomenological investigations. The aim of this series is "to demonstrate the fruitfulness of an existential-phenomenological approach to psychology." The policy statement of the series reads: "Phenomenological and existential philosophical thought is used as a basis for constructing an alternative paradigm for the practice of psychology— one that purports to do justice to human phenomena. Thus, it is hoped that it will be possible to articulate a human scientific paradigm for the praxis of psychology."

Northwestern University Press

The series published by Northwestern University Press, *Studies in Phenomenology and Existential Philosophy*, includes original works as well as translations of important French, German, and Italian books in phenomenological and existential philosophies. Thanks to this series, some classics of these philosophies have been made available in the English language for the first time. The series is thoroughly edited and supervised by an editorial board composed of high-ranking scholars from America and abroad. The first general editor of the series was John Wild.

PROSPECTS AND EVALUATION

Philosopher Bruce Wilshire (1968) considers phenomenology highly relevant to modern psychology. He thinks that the chief value of phenomenology "is that it raises a challenge to dominant modes of psychology and supplies an alternative mode of thought that keeps open vast reaches of western civilization which are in danger of being sealed off by contemporary science." In his book *William James and Phe-*

nomenology (1968), Wilshire discussed the benefits which phenomenology can bring to psychological thought and investigations.

The relevance of the phenomenological viewpoint and its compatibility with the objectivistic and scientific character of psychology have been frequent themes of articles and books published after 1960. In his book *Psychology as a Human Science* (1970), Amedeo Giorgi (b. 1931) offered a re-evaluation of the science of psychology from the phenomenological point of view. After sound training and extensive research in experimental psychology, Giorgi turned his energies to theoretical problems in psychology, particularly to the examination of the value of the phenomenological approach for scientific psychology. His articles and edited works are devoted to this problem. In the above book he proposed the thesis that psychology can and should be a science of man based on phenomenology, and that this may be accomplished by broadening the concepts of both science and objectivity.

Research Program

In his discussion of phenomenology at the First Banff Conference on Theoretical Psychology, David Krech (1970) stressed the need for two kinds of studies. One kind should set down the best procedures for obtaining useful phenomenological descriptions; the second should experimentally determine the degree of reliability and repeatability that can be expected with these procedures. "For every method in science," Krech said, "we must know *how* reliable it is. I am afraid that until both of these types of studies are done psychologists will shy away from using a method which, in my opinion, can be the beginning of wisdom *re* matters psychological."

Phenomenologists are seriously concerned with the problem of methodology. Giorgi has often addressed himself to this issue and to the entire praxis of phenomenology, as he calls it. Discussing the matter in "Toward Phenomenologically Based Research in Psychology" (1970), he responded to those who think that integration of phenomenology and experimental psychology is intrinsically impossible or that phenomenological methodology is too limited and not comprehensive enough. He took issue in particular with Brody and Oppenheim (1966, 1967), who contrasted methods of behaviorism with those of phenomenology and concluded that phenomenological psychology was irrelevant for scientific psychology. Giorgi stressed the relevance of phenomenologically based psychology and argued "that experiments in human psychology would be even better if they were based on a phenomenological perspective." He reiterated his fundamental thesis that "it is possible to conduct precise and rigorous experiments within the framework of phenomenological psychology even though different means of executing precision and rigor will have to be invented."

Spiegelberg (1972a) voiced "guarded and conditional" optimism regarding the future of phenomenological psychology and psychiatry. He looks for solid research projects, development and application of critical standards, and adequate training of qualified workers. He suggests broad research programs in the descriptive phenomenology of the life-worlds. Such programs, he feels, may aid specific psychological and psychiatric research, particularly in the areas of ego psychology, motivation, and social psychology. MacLeod (1970b) drew up a list of dimensions which emerge in phenomenological analysis and which invite further study. His subsequent feeling was that psychological phenomenology should concentrate on the phenomenal dimensions of subjectivity-objectivity and reality-irreality (1970a). "There are facts to be gleaned, and the psychologist is the one who should glean them," he wrote.

CONCLUSION

Phenomenological psychology is an orientation now well-recognized in American psychology. It is gaining wider support as a theoretical as well as a research enterprise. It is, however, decidedly popular only among a minority in America—a "counter-prescription," to use Robert I. Watson's (1965) term, with insignificant representation at universities and limited productivity, both literary and experimental. Phenomenological psychology probably has a much larger circle of sympathizers than active committed members. The progress and success of phenomenological psychology will ultimately depend not on the strength of its arguments against dominant prescriptions but on the quality and quantity of its factual, methodological, and conceptual contributions. As R. Jessor (1961) said, "Slaying the behaviorist dragon is no longer sufficient to gain the laurels of phenomenological knighthood. Only hard work will do." More than a decade has elapsed since this warning was sounded. Has it been effectively and sufficiently heeded? It appears that for phenomenological psychology to become and remain a viable movement and an enriching influence within psychology, it will have to: (1) accept some common conceptual core or proclaim some phenomenological creed which would identify and unify the dispersed phenomenological family; (2) develop and constantly improve phenomenological methodology; (3) be ever-cognizant of scientific advances in all psychological fields; (4) maintain a continuous dialogue with other psychological movements; and (5) remain in close touch with phenomenological philosophy. An interaction between philosophy and psychology will be healthy and profitable for both domains. For psychology, this interaction will hopefully provide new inspirations, open new directions of research, and, most importantly, buttress the conceptual and theoretical structure of phenomenological psychology.

SUMMARY

American phenomenological psychology owes its early inspiration to European phenomenology, both philosophical and psychological. The American branch received new impetus from the immigration of European scholars in the 1930s and after World War II who represented the Gestalt school, phenomenological philosophy, and the existential approach. The following European-born scholars were presented in some detail: Kurt Goldstein, Erwin Straus, and Aron Gurwitsch. Arguments advanced by skeptics and opponents of phenomenology were contrasted with those of the supporters of phenomenology. Several contributions to specific areas of phenomenological psychology were reviewed, namely, to perception, personality theory and research, clinical psychology, and the present direction of American psychology. Programs for research and prospects for phenomenology were considered.

American Representatives of the Phenomenological Theory:

Donald Snygg (1904-1967)
Arthur W. Combs (b. 1912)
Robert B. MacLeod (1907-1972)
Magda Arnold (b. 1903)
Mary Henle (b. 1913)
Alfred E. Kuenzli (b. 1923)
Joseph Lyons (b. 1918)
Amedeo Giorgi (b. 1931)

Chronology

1941   First plea for a phenomenological system of psychology is presented by D. Snygg in his article, "The Need for a Phenomenological System of Psychology," in the *Psychological Review.*

1947   MacLeod's article, "Phenomenological Approach to Social Psychology," appears in the *Psychological Review*.

1949   *Individual Behavior: A New Frame of Reference for Psychology* is written, by D. Snygg and A. W. Combs.

1959   *The Phenomenological Problem*, a collection of articles edited by A. E. Kuenzli, is published, and the second edition of *Individual Behavior* by D. Snygg and A. W. Combs appears.

1963   A symposium on behaviorism and phenomenology is held at Rice University.

1971   *Journal of Phenomenological Psychology* is founded and the first volume of *Studies of Phenomenological Psychology* appears.

1972   *Phenomenology in Psychology and Psychiatry: A Historical Introduction* by Herbert Spiegelberg is published.

SUGGESTED READINGS

For general information about phenomenological psychology, consult the works by MacLeod, Giorgi, Strasser, and Wann which are listed in the bibliography.

For James's phenomenology, see:

Linschoten (1970), MacLeod (1969), Spiegelberg (1972b), and Wilshire (1968).

For the effect of European immigration on American psychology, see:

Mandler & Mandler (1968), and Wellek (1968).

For controversy on phenomenological and behavioristic methodologies, see:

initial article by Brody & Oppenheim (1966), responses by Henle & Baltimore (1967), Zaner (1967), and rebuttal by Brody & Oppenheim (1967).

For controversy on the Rice Symposium on *Behaviorism and Phenomenology,* see:

Hitt (1969) and responses by Groman (1970), Egan (1970), and Sardello (1970); also a longer article on Skinner and Sartre by Kvale & Grenness (1967).

4

Existentialism and Psychology

Closely related to the effects of the phenomenological movement on psychology is the impact of the existentialist movement on psychology. Like the phenomenological movement, the existential movement also grew out of a philosophy—existential philosophy. It is therefore logical to consider first, if only generally, the origins, basic concepts, and chief exponents of this philosophy. The seeds of existentialism are found in the middle of the nineteenth century in the writings of the Danish religious thinker, Søren Kierkegaard. Existentialism's crystallization as a philosophical movement, however, took place between the two world wars in continental Europe. The principal founders of existential philosophy were two Germans, Martin Heidegger and Karl Jaspers. In France, notable representatives of this philosophy have been Gabriel Marcel, Jean-Paul Sartre, Maurice Merleau-Ponty, Paul Ricoeur, Albert Camus, and Simone de Beauvoir. In Spain, José Ortega y Gasset is the best-known exponent. And in America, an early exponent of existential thought was the prominent theologian Paul Tillich.

World War II intensified interest in existentialism. After the war, existentialism developed into a powerful cultural movement which made itself felt in virtually all aspects of contemporary life and culture. Maurice Friedman in *The Worlds of Existentialism* described existentialism as "a powerful stream, welling up from underground sources, converging and diverging, but flowing forward and carrying with it many of the most important intellectual tendencies and literary and cultural manifestations of our day." Vigorous in its expansion on the European continent for some time, existentialism has now captured the attention of the Anglo-American world and gained sympathetic audiences in various fields, including psychology. "For good or ill," William Barrett (1964) said, "existentialism has taken an acknowledged place among the more significant modes of thought within the modern world."

The borders between phenomenology and existentialism are often blurred, as the two movements conceptually interact and reinforce one another. Thus the distinction between phenomenologists and existentialists, and also the difference between phenomenological and existential contributions to psychology, are often artificial and arbitrary. For instance, the Dutch philosopher and psychologist Buytendijk, whom we discussed as a phenomenologist, could just as logically be considered in this chapter. On the other hand, Jean-Paul Sartre, for good reason, could have been mentioned in the discussion of phenomenology. Nevertheless, mostly for didactic reasons, to help students distinguish between the two philosophical strands and their differential impacts on various aspects of psychology, we shall discuss the existential movement and its influence on psychology in this, a separate chapter. American psychologists have tended to be selective in their philosophical preferences, some showing a greater inclination toward a phenomenological framework, others toward an existential movement. In general, clinical psychologists and psychotherapists have been attracted by the existential conceptualizations and borrowed themes and ideas from the existentialists more readily.

EXISTENTIALISM AS PHILOSOPHY

Husserl provided much of the initial stimulation for existentialist philosophers such as Heidegger, Sartre, and Merleau-Ponty, but the main stream of existential philosophy turned to a direction different from that which Husserl charted. While Husserl's philosophy was concerned with the essences of things, the main theme for existentialists has become *existence*. For many contemporary existentialists, phenomenology was the starting point and the first phase of their philosophical evolution. Some, notably the French existentialists, have retained closer association with phenomenology than others, such as the Germans. All existentialists, however, have accepted the phenomenological method as a basic, valid method. In this sense it can be said that existentialists are phenomenologists, but not vice versa.

Although the historical origin of existential philosophy owes much to phenomenology, its essential inspirations are derived from elsewhere, in the thought of Kierkegaard, Friedrich Nietzsche (1844-1900), and even earlier thinkers. This new movement sprang up simultaneously and yet independently in various countries and spread rapidly. The similarity of the intellectual climate and the coincidental simultaneous existence of common factors and conditions explain the origin of existentialism and its wide appeal in so many countries.

Complexity of Existential Philosophy

Existential philosophy, also called existentialist philosophy or philosophy of existence, is not a homogeneous doctrine. It is a philosophical movement comprising philosophies divergent in assumptions, conceptualization, and scope of problems. In fact, the differences among these philosophies exceed their similarities even to a higher degree than among phenomenological philosophies. The existential philosophies have, however, a common basic preoccupation, namely, existence. Existence—that is, existence as experienced by man as an individual— is the reason for the common existentialist label. The label *existentialist* first appeared in the 1920s but it did not come into general use as a designation of the philosophy of existence until the 1940s. The French existential philosophers such as Sartre and the early Marcel accepted this designation. However, the Germans, such as Heidegger and Jaspers, rejected it.

Popular notions often associate existentialism with the Parisian bistros or with bohemians. Some people think of it as a rebellion against contemporary culture or social order, or as an expression of a radical break with tradition. Whatever the motive in individual cases, the essence of existentialism and the key to its comprehension lies in its conceptual substrate, that is, in existential philosophy itself. This philosophy, it must be emphasized, is a highly technical and complex philosophy which can be neither easily summarized nor readily grasped. Its chief spokesmen, especially Heidegger and Sartre, are professional philosophers whose philosophical works are intellectually accessible only to those who are trained in abstract and speculative discourse and who are also thoroughly schooled in the history of philosophy. For example, Sartre's major work, *L'Être et le néant* (*Being and Nothingness*) is difficult even for those well-versed in philosophical literature. Mainly through Sartre's novels, plays, and essays—media which render his philosophy somewhat intelligible to the average reader—Sartre enjoys his popularity and influence. An additional source of difficulty for readers of existential writings is the unusual language abounding in neologisms. Reading philosophical works of the existentialists may be, therefore, a discouraging experience. "If one reads the existentialists without exasperation one is almost certainly misreading them," observed the translators of Bocheński's *Contemporary European Philosophy*. The length of some of these works, exemplified by Jaspers's 1947 *Philosophische Logik* (*Philosophical Logic*) whose first volume consists of 1,103 pages, also makes the reading of existentialist literature an arduous task. If existential writings are read in translation, the translator's inaccuracies or use of terms differing in meaning from that of the original language—as does occur—may render the comprehension of the author's thought much more difficult and add to the reader's exasperation.

In view of the diversity and complexity of existentialist thought, a summary of existentialism, which is attempted in this chapter, is bound to be both fragmentary and incomplete. Facing the dilemma of either omitting an account of existential philosophy altogether or giving an elementary and hence oversimplified version of it, the authors chose the latter course. Hopefully a summary of existential thought will serve as an introduction to a further study of existentialism and will, at least, call attention to those of its ideas relevant to psychology.

Departure from the Philosophical Past

Like any new philosophical movement, existentialism is best understood when examined in relation to the doctrines it has opposed. The *raison d'être* of every new philosophical doctrine lies primarily in dissatisfaction with other doctrines. Existentialism, particularly, is best comprehended if viewed as a vigorous and passionate attack against the entrenched views and main directions of the entire Western philosophical tradition.

Existentialism reacted against the rationalism of Hegel (1770-1831), bringing out instead the nonrational aspects of human nature. It also rejected positivism, materialism, and pragmatism. It opposed the Newtonian concept of an orderly, predictable world governed by immutable laws—a concept which entirely left out the human person and his specific problems. At the same time, it repudiated scientism, which conceived the world as being composed of parts that could be identified and separately analyzed and which are subject to the law of cause and effect. Above all, existentialism directed its attention not to the essence of things—thus far the main focus of science and philosophy—but to existence, to man's individual existence in particular. While proceeding in this direction, existentialism also intentionally bypassed or overcame the distinction of subject and object—a distinction inherent in all modern Western philosophy and a perennial source of its debates and division.

Existence

Although philosophy has distinguished between essence and existence and has been concerned with the essence-existence relationship, its principal interest has been traditionally in essence, that is, in what things are, rather than in their being or in existence as such. Essence has been described as "that which makes things what they are." Essence determines all characteristics and properties of things, whatever gives them their existence and stability. Existentialists—and Sartre is especially emphatic about this—deny that essence is primary and that it precedes existence. It is true, of course, that in human creations essence may precede existence, as in the case of a table made by a carpenter. He has to have a concept of a table, of its dimensions and properties, and according to this concept, he constructs the table. Here the essence precedes and determines existence. But when it comes to all nature, particularly to the individual man, his being in the world and his personal characteristics are not seen by the existentialists as determined by a prior idea. Man does not *possess* existence like the table does, he *is* his existence. All his characteristics and properties are the consequence of his existence. It is his existence that is to him the only real concrete thing, everything else being only an abstraction. This notion of human existence as experienced subjectively by man is the core of existential philosophy. If existentialist philosophers go beyond the experienced existence to engage in the metaphysics of existence, as Heidegger did, their point of departure and reference is nevertheless always human existence.

Human Existence

Existentialists interpret existence in accordance with the etymology of this word. The Latin word *exsisto,* I exist, is composed of *ex* and *sistere,* meaning literally to stand out, or to become, to emerge. That is how the existentialists understand human existence—not as merely static being, always the same, but as becoming, continually changing, developing. Man is said to be thrust in the world and necessarily and irrevocably bound to it. This notion is one of the basic axioms of existential philosophy. This notion also points to the root of man's *existential* problems, analysis of which is the central subject of existentialist writings.

The two main problems of man's existence are "the other man" and God. Man is constantly in some regard, or in relation, to other men, upon which his being, according to some existentialists, is contingent. Heidegger describes this relatedness to others as "togetherness" (*Mitsein*); Jaspers as "communication"; and Marcel as the "I" and "thou" relationship. Marcel sees men bound by love and communion with one another. Sartre describes the "other" man as enemy and his regard as menacing and degrading. The last words of Sartre's play *No Exit* are: "Hell it's the others." With respect to God, there are wide differences among existentialists. While Sartre is unequivocally atheistic, Marcel is positively theistic, and others are ambivalent or ambiguous. Martin Buber (1878-1965) brings together the two notions of God and the other man when he says that "the love of God is unreal unless it is crowned with love for one's fellow men." The pages that follow present the views of the chief exponents of existential thought.

EXISTENTIAL PHILOSOPHERS

Many philosophers who have been called existentialists reject this appellation, as was mentioned, but historians of philosophy, for good reason, continue to apply this name to such philosophers as Martin Heidegger and Karl Jaspers in Germany, and to Gabriel Marcel, Jean-Paul Sartre, and Maurice Merleau-Ponty in France.

As will be seen, existential writings differ profoundly not only in philosophical content but also in style. But they have some common features. Existential authors usually take note of one another and are prompt to spell out and emphasize their differences and agreements with other existential writers; they often appeal to human emotions and sentiments and generally to human experiences; they make frequent references to and draw upon literature—novels, plays, and poetry. The French existentialists in particular have skillfully used literary forms to communicate their views and feelings. Marcel, Sartre, Camus, and de Beauvoir have done it successfully and have attained significant standing in French literary circles.

The founders of the existential thought—Jaspers particularly—were influenced by, and acknowledged their intellectual indebtedness to, Søren Kierkegaard (1813-1855), one of the most interesting intellectuals and fascinating men of the nineteenth century, whom Walter

Lowrie (1938), his biographer, called the "grandfather" or the "great-uncle" of existentialism.

Søren Kierkegaard

The life of this Danish thinker was short—only 42 years—but of far-reaching consequences: he stirred up the minds and hearts of many great men of many countries and is still widely read and discussed. A well-to-do man, he acquired a thorough training in philosophy, which he studied in Berlin at the time of Hegel. He worked in the field of journalism for a time and then spent the rest of his life in solitude, meditating and writing. His books, among which the most outstanding are, in their English titles, *Either/Or, The Concept of Dread* and *The Sickness unto Death,* became famous only after 1909 when they were translated into other languages. Kierkegaard thought of himself as a "religious author," yet he was admired not so much for his theological ideas as for his penetrating analysis of man's inner experiences, or—to put him in relation to existential thought—man's existential problems. He was, in fact, perhaps the first to use the term "existence" in the sense that existentialists are using it now.

The main theme of Kierkegaard's works is man and his conflicts. He views man as constantly desiring eternity, to be as eternal as God Himself, but yet clearly realizing that his existence is temporal and finite. He wants to escape from his finitude but cannot. Man then defends himself from the thought of eternity. He tries to forget it by desperately occupying himself with trivialities and temporal things so that his mind will not have time to think about eternity and God. The conflict between these two opposing forces, toward eternity and toward temporality—the conflict arising from the finite man confronting infinite God—stirs in man torment, anguish, and dread. Kierkegaard gave an account of this experience in *The Concept of Dread.* It has been said that nothing comparable to this genuine, moving, and profound account can be found in any literature. The history of Kierkegaard's inner life, recounted by him in detail in his books and diaries, offers rich insights into human nature.

Martin Heidegger

Heidegger (b. 1889) owes his philosophical formation to several thinkers, but principally to Husserl and Kierkegaard. His association with Husserl was mentioned in Chapter 1. After he left the chair of philosophy at Freiburg, Heidegger retired to a remote place in the Black Forest to devote himself entirely to his philosophical work. He is recognized as an original and brilliant thinker. At the same time, however, he is perhaps the most difficult contemporary philosopher to read and follow because of his unusual terminology comprised of German, Latin, and Greek words. His chief work, *Sein und Zeit* (1927; English translation, *Being and Time,* 1962) has been of particular significance for psychology and psychiatry. Several existential psychologists and psychiatrists in Europe have drawn upon it, as they did upon Heidegger's published lecture *What is Metaphysics?* (1929) and a *Postscript* to it written 18 years later. W. J. Richardson's comprehensive book, *Heidegger: Through Phenomenology to Thought* (1963), to which Heidegger himself wrote a preface, traced the evolution of this philosopher's system and analyzed its present status. The same author discussed Heidegger's relation to humanism and relevance to humanistic psychology (1971).

Human existence (*Dasein*), Heidegger teaches, is tied inseparably to the world (*being-in-the-world,* as the English translators render this idea) and to other human beings. Of all beings, only man is aware of his existence. He realizes that his existence is not of his making or a consequence of his choice, but that it has been thrust upon him, and it will be his lot until his death. Finding himself thrown into this incomprehensible and threatening world, as Heidegger describes it, and among strange people, and discovering his life oriented toward inescapable death, man experiences dread and anguish. This experience Heidegger describes in great detail. Man tries to overcome dread, Heidegger says, by camouflaging it with life which is conventional and "inauthentic." Man's thoughts, acts, and speech conform to the conventional modes of thinking, acting, and speaking. He thinks and does what "one" usually thinks or does. He thinks, for instance, that "one has to die," but he does not allow himself to think that it is he himself who has to die. But there is a price man has to pay for evading the realities of his being, for this camouflaging. It is a feeling of guilt which pervades his entire being. Thus only by accepting the inevitability of death and nothingness can man be true to himself, that is, can man have an authentic existence and be genuinely free. Only few succeed in living an authentic existence, and those who do have to defend it constantly against the clutches of the conventional, inauthentic modes of existence. It is this concept that some psychiatrists—particularly the Swiss psychiatrist, Ludwig Binswanger—elaborated and applied to the field of psychotherapy.

Jean-Paul Sartre

None of the existentialist philosophers is better known than Sartre (b. 1905). Mainly because of his novels, plays, and articles which popularized his ideas that existentialism was, to some, synonymous with Sartre's philosophy. Before World War II Sartre was a teacher of philosophy. He studied German phenomenology—and psychoanalysis—during his two-year stay in Berlin. During the war, he served in the French army and was taken prisoner by the Germans. When he was released, he joined the French underground movement. Since the war his activities have varied, including journalism, editorship of a magazine, politics, and, most important, publication of philosophical books, novels, and plays. Sartre stirred up public opinion when he refused the Nobel Prize for literature in 1964.

Sartre's first publications were concerned with psychological subjects, mainly imagination and emotions. The book which established his place in philosophy was *L'Être et le néant* (1943; English translation, *Being and Nothingness,* 1956).

The central question for Sartre has revolved around the meaning of man's existence. What is this meaning? Sartre's striking answer is that man's and world's existence have no meaning at all: No reason can be found to explain why the world and man in it should exist at all. If God existed, an explanation would be possible, but there is no God; according to Sartre, there is not even the possibility of God. Sartre considers the very concept of God a contradiction. Thus the world with all the beings has no justification, no sense; it is absurd. Of all the beings, man is the most inexplicable because of his consciousness, which is an undeniable reality and yet incomprehensible as to its origin and continuity. Sartre's phrase, "man is a useless passion," has become almost an earmark of his philosophy.

According to Sartre, what characterizes man best is his freedom and capability of choice. This freedom is not merely a quality or an attribute that he possesses. Rather, man *is* freedom, and he therefore has to choose and decide all the time. Since he inevitably has to bear all the consequences of his decisions, his freedom is an awesome yoke. As Sartre puts it, man is condemned to be free. Man is what he decides to make of himself; his mode of existence is his choice. If he tries to escape his freedom, he is gripped by nausea, anxiety, forlornness, and despair.

The springboard of Sartre's philosophy was phenomenology. The subtitle of *Being and Nothingness* is characteristic: "An Outline of Phenomenological Ontology." The phenomenological approach is evident in Sartre's psychological discussions, especially in his study of imagination and emotion. Finding the existing theories on imagination unsatisfactory, he wrote *L'Imagination* (*Imagination*, 1936), a phenomenological analysis of this process. Later he undertook this analysis in *L'Imaginaire: psychologie phénoménologique de l'imagination* (1940; translated into English as *Psychology of Imagination*). Emotions were another subject of his phenomenological analysis. In *Esquisse d'une théorie des émotions* (1939; in English, *The Emotions: Outline of a Theory*), he discussed their nature and significance. Emotions are "a certain way of apprehending the world," he said. Their purpose is to transform the real world, when it becomes too difficult to handle in certain situations, into an unreal one, into a magical world, conferring on it qualities which it actually does not possess. In his description of fear, for example, he speaks of fainting from fear as "a refuge." "Lacking the power to avoid the danger, I denied it" by fainting or fleeing.

There is an extensive chapter in *Being and Nothingness* on existential psychoanalysis. It was published in English separately as *Existential Psychoanalysis* (1953). This is not Freudian psychoanalysis, but Sartre's own method of finding the value system adopted by the patient. This value system can be found by the analysis of a patient's behavior. Since, as Sartre teaches, each individual chooses what he wants to be and since as a man he is a unified whole, he expresses his choice in every aspect of his behavior. An analysis of his behavioral acts should therefore reveal what his original choice was. When this choice is revealed to the patient, he will usually recognize it. The patient may, however, deceive himself; he may be, as Sartre calls it, "of bad faith" and may not acknowledge his original true choice. It is then up to the psychoanalyst to reveal to the patient what his choice had been and also the fact of his being in "bad faith." Sartre applied his psychoanalysis to the study of literary men—Baudelaire, Flaubert, Genet—and even to himself, in the autobiographical book, *Les Mots* (English translation, *The Words,* 1964).

This brief account of Sartre's views has been selective. Sartre has dealt with many other problems of man and society. His thought on various issues is still evolving, and occasionally he modifies or reformulates his earlier views. *The Words,* his first autobiographical volume (his life up to the age of 12), sounded to many almost like a recantation of his previous position concerning the value of words and literature. Once showing a great passion for words, reading, and writing, Sartre appeared in this book utterly disillusioned with the usefulness of his own writings and of all literature. This French philosopher obviously has not yet said his final word, but the effect of his philosophy has already left a deep mark on contemporary thought.

Gabriel Marcel

Unlike most existential philosophers, Marcel (b. 1889) has developed his philosophy independently of Husserl and other phenomenologists. He put forth existentialist concepts as early as 1914. Marcel shares many features with other existentialist thinkers such as Heidegger and Jaspers, but the tone of his philosophy—hopeful and optimistic— and his theism are in striking contrast with theirs, particularly with Sartre's. Like Sartre, he is a playwright and literary critic and has found a wide and receptive audience in France and elsewhere. For a time Marcel called himself a "Christian existentialist," but in 1951 he emphatically renounced any existentialist designation of his philosophy. He has traveled extensively, acquired a profound knowledge of world literature, and has been in contact with well-known personalities in political and literary life.

Marcel has not written any systematic exposition of his entire philosophy, preferring instead to deal with single issues separately. His major work, *Journal métaphysique* (1927; English translation, *Metaphysical Journal*), contains analyses of several problems. Books such as *Homo Viator* (*Man the Wayfarer,* 1945) or *Le Mystère de l'être* (1951; English translation, *The Mystery of Being,* 2 vols.) are devoted to analyses of a variety of human experiences and to meditations on topics such as art, technology, and fatherhood. *L'Homme problématique* (1955; English translation, *Problematic Man,* 1967) is composed of two parts. The first part reflects on the basic problems which pertain to the meaning of life and which man desperately tries to solve for himself. The second part has twelve chapters exploring human uneasiness and ways of understanding and dealing with it.

The realm of thought for which Marcel is best known pertains to man-to-man relationship. The key word to the understanding of his thought on this subject is *being-by-participation.* Man comes into his individual being, Marcel says, by communion with other men through love, hope, and faithfulness. The other man must not be a mere "It" or just "somebody," but "Thou," known and loved. Only through the relationship with man as "Thou" does the "I" find his freedom and fulfillment. By loving others, man transcends his own limited self. Without love, man's existence is isolated and reduced. God is the absolute "Thou" who cannot be demonstrated by rational discourse, but He is only encountered in man's personal engagement with Him.

Karl Jaspers

Jaspers (1883-1969), whom Heidegger called the founder of German existentialism, was a practicing psychiatrist before he devoted himself entirely to philosophy. In 1913, as a young resident in a psychiatric hospital in Heidelberg, he wrote a large systematic volume on psychopathology, *Allgemeine Psychopathologie* (English translation, *General Psychopathology,* 1963). The book was well received, gained Jaspers recognition in psychiatry, and was revised by the author seven times, the last in 1959. In this work Jaspers emphasizes the need for a detailed description of the patient's subjective experiences to determine a correct diagnosis and the need for empathy with the patient's feelings for a successful therapy. In the same year that his book was published, Jaspers entered academic life and devoted most of his time to lecturing, studying, and writing. He first lectured on theoretical and empirical psychology, specifically on subjects such as sense perceptions, memory, fatigue, ability, and typology of personality. Psychology, which was Jaspers's main preoccupation for several years, gradually led him to philosophy. His work *Die Psychologie der Weltanschauungen* (*Psychology of Personal Views on Life,* 1919) signaled his turning to philosophy. Jaspers held a chair of philosophy at Heidelberg before and after World War II, but from 1948 until his death he was professor of philosophy at the University in Basel, Switzerland. This was his longest and last academic appointment. He presented his philosophical views in a systematic manner in his three-volume *Philosophie* (*Philosophy,* 1932). The number and scope of his publications surpass those of contemporary existentialists. He has also been the most consistent and comprehensible of all the existential philosophers.

Jaspers has been concerned with all great traditional philosophical problems, but especially with all aspects of being. His aim was to provide a philosophy—or, as he preferred to call it, "a mode of observation"—which would encompass the entire spectrum of problems related to man's existence. He distinguished three forms or modes of being: *being-there, being-oneself,* and *being-in-itself.* Being-there is the objective empirical world, which we come to know through observation and experiment. Being-oneself is the personal existence, depending on our awareness of ourselves and our liberty and on our assertion of ourselves by choice and decisions. Being-in-itself is the world in its transcendence. Philosophy has to keep these forms distinct and explore them through appropriate methods, but man can participate in all three at once. But even then, man can never fathom the entire meaning of existence.

Man is continually self-becoming through realization of his liberty and through his decisions, Jaspers maintained. He must constantly judge himself in the light of these decisions. Confronted with inescapable situations such as death, suffering, struggle, and guilt, man has to deal with them all alone. He is not isolated from the rest of the world, however, but is in constant communication with other existences. This communication is constitutive of his own existence—that is, he exists because he is in communication with others. There are various forms of communication, such as discussion, social intercourse, ruling and serving, and political relations. Communication between systems of thought is essential for philosophy, because no philosophical system can possess entire and ultimate truth.

Jaspers was not impressed by empirical psychology's character and achievements. He thought that scientific psychology, despite all its intense research efforts, could never hope to arrive at a comprehensive and valid grasp of human nature as it lacked proper methodology to do this. Dissatisfied with the naturalistic scientific tendency of the psychology of his day, he formulated his own brand of psychology which he called *verstehende Psychologie* ("understanding psychology"). This psychology, which received much attention in Germany, was later developed into a system in a book, *Verstehende Psychologie* (1948) by Jaspers's friend and former medical colleague at the Heidelberg mental hospital who was once the sharpest though benevolent critic of *Psychopathology,* Hans W. Gruhle (1880-1958). But for Jaspers this psychology was merely a temporary station in his climb to broader philosophical perspectives, toward his existentialism. He returned to psychology only occasionally, notably in his psychological biographies of Strindberg and van Gogh (1922), four revisions of his *Psychologie der Weltanschauungen,* and in several critical reports on work in neurology, psychiatry, and psychology (until 1921). As he later stated, Jaspers did not feel it necessary to correct his psychological and psychiatric views much, whereas he constantly worked over his philosophical thought. As the years passed, he grew more absorbed with philosophical problems. When Jaspers was 74, he concluded in his intellectual autobiography:

> One's consciousness is agitated by the fact that one has not yet said the essential thing, not yet found what announces itself. For this reason a philosophical retrospect becomes a better plan for future work. The expansive power of reason is not enclosed in the biological circle of life. One may get into the mood—paradoxical for old age—that, by virtue of one's spiritual experiences, the vision opens to new distances.

General Comments

The above accounts are too brief and too selective to do justice to the diversity and depth of existential thought. They were intended to exemplify the basic feature of existentialism, namely, its concern with the question of human individual existence and its ultimate meaning. But existentialism, it is clear enough, has not offered one comprehensive answer to this question. There are as many answers as there are forms of existential thought.

Existentialism is an attempt to deal seriously and squarely with problems which philosophy had thus far neglected. Traditional Western philosophy has concentrated almost exclusively on the metaphysics of being, essences, man's rational nature, and the external objective world. It has thus bypassed man's emotions and his burning questions of the meaning of life, suffering, and death. The individual man, with his unique individual problems of everyday existence and the basic existential problems shared by all men, has been left out of philosophical inquiries. Existentialism, reacting to this deficiency, centers its attention on man as he exists in the world and on his relation to the world and to his fellow men. This reaction, as we have already noted, appeared in various countries and in many fields simultaneously and yet independently. Such a phenomenon may be explained in terms of common conflicts and anxieties which have arisen in the Western world in the last 100 years and which have been intensified by the global wars and the threat of annihilation by nuclear explosion. These conflicts and anxieties are also believed to account for the upsurge in the Western world of interest in some Oriental philosophical and religious systems such as Lao-Tzu and Zen Buddhism, systems which contain elements akin to existentialism. Apparently the Western man finds or hopes to find—be it in such Oriental movements or in existentialism—ideas and answers which could allay his anxieties, give him understanding of himself, and make it possible for him to discover the meaning of life.

Existentialism as a philosophy has put itself in opposition to materialistic reductionism, idealism, and rationalism. In attacking these doctrines, however, existentialism has perhaps gone too far in the opposite direction and has left by the wayside the objective and scientific elements of philosophy. Some critics say that if the proposition of some existentialists—namely, that there are no universal truths or laws—were correct, the construction of science would be impossible. Other objections leveled at existential philosophers include: excessive subjectivism (relying on personal subjective experiences as the basis for conclusions, without any attempt of proof or demonstration), lack of a springboard for decision and action, the categorical tone of existentialist pronouncements, and uncommunicative esoteric language. This last characteristic has been the object of vehement criticism of neopositivists, who insist on precision of expression and definitions. They deride the vague and peculiar parlance of some existential writers. Their special target has been Heidegger, for such expressions as "nothingness makes nought" (*das Nichts selbst nichtet*).

These characteristics of existentialism have been part of the reason why American philosophers and psychologists too were indifferent to existentialist philosophy for many years. The intellectual climate of America, where neopositivism and pragmatism have dominated and where rigorous scientific methodology has been demanded, was not conducive to the study of existentialism and contributed to its delay. But the situation has changed, and since the 1950s existentialism has been studied and discussed in America. Indeed it has found influential supporters and able interpreters.

There is a general agreement in nonpartisan circles that whatever its exaggerations and deficiencies, existentialism has opened new horizons for philosophical inquiry and awakened man's reflection in a new and vital direction. Existentialism has forced philosophers and psychologists to re-examine their notions about man and his nature and to take a stand with regard to man's existential problems. On the other hand, it is also generally agreed that it would be an exaggeration to contend that existentialist thinking is the only legitimate approach in philosophy and that the existential issues are the only issues worthy of philosophical study.

EXISTENTIAL PSYCHOLOGY

Favorable conditions have always existed in Europe for the penetration of novel philosophical ideas into psychology, as we have pointed out before. The two disciplines, philosophy and psychology, have traditionally remained in close contact. An average European intellectual has some training in philosophy because university curricula demand it from most students. Also, characteristically, he is interested in new philosophical currents. This is particularly true of psychologists who, as a rule, are better versed than the average educated person in philosophy, especially in the history of philosophy. It is therefore understandable that such a powerful and psychologically oriented movement as existentialism readily influenced European psychological thought, especially in quarters where phenomenology had already prepared the ground for such an influence. Phenomenologically-minded psychologists were attuned and well disposed to existentialism; thus they were often the first to espouse existentialist concepts and weave them into their psychologies.

Existential psychology, as it began to emerge in Europe, did not aspire to be an all-exclusive new form of psychology, nor even a new theory or branch of psychology. Rather, it viewed itself as a new orientation or a new perspective, essentially idiographic, different from the nomothetic tendencies of other forms of psychology. Its intention has been not to abolish the existing tendencies and approaches of modern psychology but to complement them by introducing another viewpoint and new themes and methods, which were either missing altogether in traditional psychology or up to now have not been given sufficient attention.

European Existential Psychologists

The existential approach to psychology developed on the European continent into a distinct movement in the 1940s, almost simultaneously with the philosophical movement. It steadily grew more articulate and influential. Confined for a while to continental Europe and noticed in America only when it was well advanced, this movement has quickly become international. It now has followers among psychologists and psychiatrists of every western European country. It is to be noted, though, that existential psychology in Europe is far from homogeneous in its character and orientation. Its representatives show wide differences in conceptualization, interests, and emphases.

F. J. Buytendijk, whom we have already discussed in Chapter 2, described existential psychology as being based "on the primordial fact of human existence" and consisting "first and foremost" in the analysis of the meaning-structures of the personal world toward which all activity is directed. In his opinion the best way to know man is "to study the dialogue of man with objects and with his fellow-men." "It is impossible to know an individual," he says, "without taking his personal world into account."

Characteristics of Existential Psychology

The existential approach in psychology is still historically new and not sufficiently systematized to permit a comprehensive account of its development or its precise definition. The following points specify those characteristics which apply to the movement as a whole rather than to its individual representatives and should be regarded as tentative formulations of viewpoints expressed by various writers on different occasions.

1. Existential psychology, inspired by existential philosophy, is not a school but a *movement,* which focuses its inquiry on man as an individual person as being-in-the-world (the hyphenation indicates the inseparability of being and the world). It seeks to bring into psychology a new viewpoint, new themes, and new methods. Van Kaam (1966) thinks of this movement as only temporary because, he says, psychology will eventually assimilate the existential viewpoint and thus become existential itself.

2. Several basic theses or presuppositions underlie this movement: (a) Every man is unique in his inner life, his perception and evaluation of the world, and his reaction to it. (b) Man as a person cannot be understood in terms of the functions or elements that make him up. Neither can he be explained in terms of physics, chemistry, or neurophysiology. (c) Psychology, if it is modeled after physics—employing exclusively objective scientific methods, working solely within the stimulus-response framework, and focused on functions such as sensation, perception, learning, drives, habits, and emotional behavior—is incapable of contributing significantly to the understanding of the nature of man. (d) Neither the behavioristic nor the psychoanalytic approach is completely satisfactory.

3. Existential psychology attempts to *complement,* not to replace or suppress, other existing orientations in psychology.

4. Its *aim* is the development of a comprehensive concept of man and the understanding of man in his total existential reality. Its approach in working toward this aim is basically idiographic—that is, it deals not with generalities applicable to any human person but with problems peculiar to this or that individual person. Its concern is with this person's consciousness, feelings, moods, and experiences related to his individual existence in the world and among other men. But its ultimate goal is to discover the basic force, theme, or tendency in human life which would provide a key to the understanding of human nature in its entirety.

5. Its frequent *themes* are man-to-man relationship, freedom and responsibility, individual scale of values, the meaning of life, suffering, anxiety, and death.

6. Its chief *method* is the phenomenological method, described in the previous chapter, consisting of the exploration of man's consciousness and subjective experiences. Existential psychology is trying to develop specific methods to be able to meaningfully study various dimensions of individual experiences.

7. The *contributions* which existential psychology has made so far are principally in the field of personality theory, psychotherapy, and counseling.

There is much conceptual and methodological overlapping and communality of aims between the existential and the phenomenological approaches. The intermingling of the phenomenological and existential philosophies may be so complete in many instances that distinctions and classification into two categories cannot be made.

EXISTENTIAL PSYCHOTHERAPY

The influence of existentialism is also strongly evident in psychiatry, psychodiagnostics, theory of mental disorders, and most particularly in psychotherapy. This influence is understandable in light of the genuine concern for the human condition and subjective experience of the individual shared by existential philosophy and psychotherapy. Moreover, the psychotherapist discovers in existential philosophy a frame of reference particularly well suited for the therapeutic situation. Hendrik M. Ruitenbeek expressed this in his introduction to *Psychoanalysis and Existential Philosophy* (1962):

> Existential philosophy . . . provides the analyst with a set of principles which can serve as guidelines in a broad general interpretation of clinical material. For existentialism approaches man's life directly. By using its concepts, the analyst can press on to the bedrock of man's existence and so establish a more immediate and fruitful relation with his patients.

New and vigorous psychotherapeutic systems and concepts, constructed on phenomenological and existential principles, have recently emerged, some of them opposing and seriously challenging the psychoanalytic system in its method and theory.

Existential Analysis

The most widely known—and undoubtedly the most influential—existential concept in psychiatry is that of the Swiss psychiatrist Ludwig Binswanger (1881-1966), who has termed it *Daseinsanalyse,* or existential analysis, a term borrowed from Heidegger. Originally a Freudian, Binswanger departed substantially from Freud when he incorporated into his concepts elements from phenomenology and existentialist philosophy, particularly from Heidegger. Existential analysis is neither a new system nor a new technique, but a new concept—Binswanger called it "a psychiatric-phenomenologic research method"—which envisages man as being-in-the-world. As such, it is not satisfied with the mere phenomenological exploration of the patient's subjective experiences but probes into his "existential modes." This means that the patient is to be understood in terms of the relationships that his "self" establishes with the world (*Umwelt*), with his fellowmen (*Mitwelt*), and with himself (*Eigenwelt*). In existential analysis, the therapist does not direct, guide, or correct the patient according to some preconceived notions; rather, he simply helps him to become his own authentic self or, in other words, to achieve a degree of self-realization capable of preserving his integrity. The psychotherapist, Binswanger said, allows the patient "to find his way back from his neurotic or psychotic, lost, erring, perforated or twisted mode of existence and world, into the freedom of being able to utilize his own capacities for existence."

Binswanger found many enthusiastic followers in Europe, but there are also opponents and critics of his existential analysis. The most objectionable aspect of Binswanger's *Daseinsanalyse* seems to be its heavy philosophical substructure and its close linkage with Heidegger's philosophy. Jaspers, who introduced phenomenology into psychiatry, finds "a philosophical and scientific error" in Binswanger's view.

Other Psychotherapeutic Approaches

There are several derivations of Heidegger's or Binswanger's *Daseinsanalyse.* "Existential analysis" now covers a number of psychopathologic and psychotherapeutic schools of thought, closely or loosely allied with Heidegger's philosophical system. There are also approaches which are not at all allied with any particular existential philosopher but only with the general core of the existential thought. One of the common features of these various approaches is the emphasis on complete exploration of the patient's consciousness and experiences, as the individual's experience rather than physical events is held to be the cause of his pathology. Since man's choices determine what he is or will be, the therapist seeks to find what his client's original or basic choice was that led to his maladjustment. Most existential therapists believe that the neurotic is not fully realizing his potentialities; therefore he must be helped to come back to the full experience of his existence.

The effort on the part of the therapist to enter into his patient's inner world, to experience what the patient experiences, is the distinctive feature of the existential approach to psychotherapy. The understanding of this inner world of the patient (especially his *Eigenwelt,* or relationship with himself) guides the clinician in selecting therapeutic measures. There is no standard therapeutic technique specific to the existential approach. In fact, representatives of this approach hold that overemphasis on technique is one of the main obstacles to understanding the patient: it is not the understanding that follows technique, but the technique that follows understanding. However, several therapeutic methods and even specific techniques have been developed. They are not practiced rigidly or indiscriminately, however. Their use depends on the individual patient, the therapeutic situation, and other considerations. It is noteworthy that some of the existential European literature which influenced psychiatry and psychotherapy has strong religious overtones reflecting the beliefs of the authors—Jewish, Catholic, and Protestant. For instance, Martin Buber drew from the Jewish tradition, Gabriel Marcel from Catholic beliefs, and Paul Tillich from his close ties with Protestant theology.

Leading Psychotherapists in Europe

There has been a large group of existential psychiatrists and psychotherapists in various countries representing a wide spectrum of viewpoints regarding psychopathology and the psychotherapeutic process. Quite individualistic and idiosyncratic was the way each of these representatives responded to the phenomenological and existential thought, what he assimilated from it, and how he used it. The result is a mosaic, whose individual pieces are difficult to identify and relate.

In Austria are Caruso and Frankl; in Britain, Laing; in France, Minkowski and H. Ey; in Germany, Gebsattel and Zutt; in Italy, Assagioli; in the Netherlands, van den Berg; in Switzerland, Binswanger, Boss, and Kuhn. These are merely examples of views which are easy to identify. The roster of psychotherapists with phenomenological and existential leanings is actually much longer.

Austria's psychiatrist Igor A. Caruso (b. 1914), Gebsattel's student, formulated a concept of "personalistic psychotherapy," which considers analysis as only the first step to the more important phase of the therapeutic process, a synthesis in which religious and moral values of the patient play an essential part. His book *Psychoanalyse und Synthese der Existenz* (1951), in which he argues in favor of such a synthesis, was translated into English in 1964—unfortunately with the grossly misleading title, *Existential Psychology: From Analysis to Synthesis.*

The French translation of Jaspers's *General Psychopathology* introduced phenomenology to French psychiatry. The first decisive turn to phenomenology appeared prominently in the psychiatric research and writings of the Polish-born psychiatrist Eugène Minkowski (1885-1972). In addition to German phenomenology, which he came to know during his studies in Germany, the philosophy of Henri Bergson and personal contacts with him shaped Minkowski's psychiatric thought. He communicated his ideas in his works on schizophrenia (1927), the experience of time and its distortions in mental illness (*Le Temps vécu,* 1933; in English, *Lived Time,* 1970), and finally in his treatise on psychopathology (1966). Minkowski was a co-founder and co-editor of an important psychopathological journal in France, *L'Évolution psychiatrique.* His psychiatric views and theories evoked international attention, especially his concept of schizophrenia, in which he stressed loss of contact with reality, autism, and morbid rationalization as the major symptoms of the disease.

Minkowski's younger colleague and collaborator in *L'Évolution psychiatrique* was Henri Ey (b. 1900), a psychiatrist and author of international reputation and influence. Ey has considerably strengthened the phenomenological-existential trend in French psychiatry, and his views found followers in psychiatric circles both in his country and abroad. In his three volumes of *Études psychiatriques* (1948-1953), he presented his views and described his studies on a wide range of topics treated in the phenomenological spirit. In building his coherent psychopathological doctrine, Ey utilized elements from phenomenology and existentialism, as well as from psychoanalysis and organic approaches of British neurologist Hughlings Jackson and Kurt Goldstein. The name of his theory of psychoses and neuroses, "organodynamic," is meant to convey its organic orientation and rejection of mechanistic outlook. Ey's existential psychiatry and French existential psychiatry in general have been relatively little known in America. Traditionally, Americans have shown more interest in German psychiatric and psychological literature than in French. An outline of Ey's organodynamic theory was made available in English in *Psychiatry and Philosophy* (1969), edited by E. Straus.

Germany's octogenarian psychiatrist Victor E. von Gebsattel (b. 1883), whose 80th birthday was celebrated by a *Festschrift* to which 34 authors contributed—among them his friends Binswanger and Erwin Straus—is not well known in America despite his influence in Europe. One of the reasons may be a lack of a systematic exposition by Gebsattel of his theories and practices. Since 1907, when he began publishing, he preferred to deal with specific topics in his books and articles than to prepare a treatise of his system, which he called "anthropological psychiatry." In his meaning of the word, "anthropological" denotes the concern with the whole man in his ontological entirety as self, personality, and person. This approach is close to that of Gebsattel's friends Binswanger and E. Straus. Binswanger characterized Gebsattel as "the most intuitive" of their trio. The importance of a personal relationship between the therapist and patient in the psychotherapeutic process—which greatly interested Gebsattel—was also of great concern to another German psychiatrist, Jürg Zutt. He described the gap initially existing between the therapist and his patient, the developing encounter between the two, and the bridging of the gap at the personal level.

Italy's Roberto Assagioli (b. 1888) has developed a system of psychotherapy which he calls psychosynthesis. Its early idea was already conceived in his doctoral dissertation in 1910 out of dissatisfaction with the limitations of Freud's views. The concept has grown into a complete theory of personality, based on the central function of the "self" and its full actualization, and a system of psychotherapy, in which art and artistic experiences play a central role. Psychosynthesis met with success in Europe and farther, proved by the formation of centers and institutes devoted to the practice of this system. The Psychosynthesis Research Foundation was created in the United States in 1957. In 1965 a book in English appeared, *Psychosynthesis,* in which Assagioli explained his system and provided a manual of his psychotherapeutic techniques.

In the Netherlands J. H. van den Berg (b. 1914), professor of psychology and phenomenological psychopathology, is well known. His books, translated from Dutch into various languages, have made him as well known as the phenomenological approach to psychiatry. His concise exposition of this approach under the clear title *The Phenomenological Approach to Psychiatry* (1955) was instrumental in arousing interest in the application of phenomenology to psychiatry in America. But he authored books which dealt with both fundamental issues and specific phenomenological areas. An example of the first type was *The Changing Nature of Man: Introduction to a Historical Psychology of Man* (1961), acclaimed by the eminent anthropologist Ashley Montagu as one of the most original and sensitive books on the nature of man to be published during the past quarter century. His latest publication available in English, *Things* (1970), discusses material objects as part of our life-world, how they are perceived by us, and how they affect us.

Switzerland's Medard Boss and Roland Kuhn have carried the banner of phenomenology and existentialism in the context of psychotherapy. Medard Boss (b. 1903), professor of psychotherapy at the

University of Zurich, has been strongly influenced by Heidegger, his personal friend. Among his more influential and better known publications are his book on sexual perversions (in English, *Meaning and Content of Sexual Perversions*, 1949), well received by psychiatric and legal circles, and another on interpretation of dreams (English translation, *The Analysis of Dreams*, 1958), in which he departed radically from Freud. Roland Kuhn (b. 1912), a close follower of Binswanger, combined psychotherapy with chemotherapy in his practice. In fact, he was responsible for the introduction of an antidepressive drug, Tofranil, now widely used in psychiatry. He also used the Rorschach test in a new way and conducted research in this area.

Logotherapy

A much discussed and one of the best known existential psychotherapeutic approaches in America has been the logotherapy of Viktor E. Frankl (b. 1905), professor on the medical faculty of the University of Vienna and head of the department of neurology at the Poliklinik Hospital in Vienna. The basic thesis of logotherapy, which is referred to as the "Third Viennese School of Psychotherapy" (the first two being those of Freud and Adler), is that man's most fundamental drive is to understand the meaning of his own existence. Frankl calls this drive the "will-to-meaning." If this drive is not fulfilled, frustration follows—"the existential frustration," which may result in a neurosis whose characteristic feature is escape from freedom and responsibility. The task of the therapist is not to provide an authoritative answer to the question "What am I for?," but to help the patient discover for himself the meaning of his personal existence and to encourage him to put this meaning to full realization. In doing this, psychotherapy restores in the patient freedom and responsibility, the two distinctive human characteristics. Underlying logotherapy is a concept of man as a spiritual being whose existence has an intrinsic meaning. This meaning, which is individual for every person, man has to find and realize in his life.

Frankl does not intend to replace other forms of therapy but to supplement them. He does not reject Freud but seeks to complement him. In *Man's Search for Meaning* (1946; new enlarged English edition with G. W. Allport's preface, 1963), one of the psychological bestsellers of enduring popularity—which contains an autobiographical account of Frankl's experiences in a Nazi concentration camp, as well as the fundamental concepts of logotherapy—he tells of his answer to the question, ". . . what is the difference between psychoanalysis and logotherapy?" Before answering, Frankl asked the man who posed the question, ". . . but in the first place, can you tell me in one sentence what you think the essence of psychoanalysis is?" The answer was, "During psychoanalysis, the patient must lie down on a couch and tell you things that sometimes are very disagreeable to tell." "Whereupon I immediately retorted," tells Frankl, "with the following improvisation: 'Now, in logotherapy the patient may remain sitting erect, but he must hear things that sometimes are very disagreeable to hear.' "

Logotherapy found followers and sympathizers both in Europe and America. Many of Frankl's 16 books were translated into European and Oriental languages. His frequent visits to America and lecture tours here made him widely known on this side of the Atlantic. A certain amount of research has been done here to test some of the theses proposed by Frankl. A psychometric instrument has been devised, the PIL (Purpose in Life), which is designed to measure the degree to which the subject has found meaningful goals around which he integrates his life.

Madness and Society

Mental illness and sanity have been examined from a new existential perspective by a practicing British psychiatrist, Ronald D. Laing (b. 1927), who has received increasing attention because of the originality and forcefulness of his writings. Equally at home with classical psychiatric literature as with existential works, Laing has extensively researched mental illness and has arrived at conclusions which he shared with the public in his controversial books—the first, *The Divided Self* (1959), and the latest, *The Politics of the Family* (1971). Laing is also a poet, and his book of poems, *Knots* (1970), has found considerable success.

Laing's research has taken him to the field of interpersonal relations, interaction processes in the families of schizophrenics, and effects of psychedelic drugs. His studies of schizophrenics led him to the conclusion that "the experience and behavior that gets labeled schizophrenic is *a special strategy that a person invents in order to live in an unlivable situation.*" What we call a "normal" and "adjusted" state "is too often," he said, "abdication of ecstasy, the betrayal of our true potentialities, that many of us are only too successful in acquiring a false self to adapt to false realities." Laing questions whether contemporary psychiatry, current therapies, and mental hospitals do any good; he instead thinks that they may be unnecessary or even harmful.

In Laing's opinion the therapist should try to penetrate his patient's façade, his "false self" which the patient erects to protect himself from disturbing life realities or from ailing society, and to reach the real person, the "inner self." To achieve this the therapist should let the illness run its course, observe it, and at the same time give the patient his devoted, sympathetic, and reassuring presence and companionship. The blame for mental illness and other ills of mankind Laing often attributes to contemporary society, which he criticizes for its inhumaneness. Accused of anti-intellectualism, glorification of schizophrenia, and destroying structures rather than proposing new ones to build upon, Laing has become the center of debates. His therapeutic approach to mental illness, many psychiatrists say, is a matter of his personal skill and mystique and is too individualistic to be useful for the profession at large. However, even his opponents concede that Laing has drawn attention to the social aspects of mental illness which have thus far been ignored, and that his studies of schizophrenics have advanced our knowledge of this illness.

Psychoanalysis and Existentialism

It is not surprising that existentialism and psychoanalysis have remained aloof, for there was no natural meeting ground between the world of the unconscious and the world of consciousness. Psychoanalysts showed little or no interest in phenomenological and existential work in psychopathology and psychotherapy, and existentialists did not attempt any dialogue with psychoanalysis, although they were, of course, aware of Freud and the psychoanalytic movement. French existentialists for the most part were an exception; they paid attention to psychoanalysis and examined it from the existential point of view. Existential psychiatrists in France—H. Ey, for example—were also more inclined to borrow ideas from psychoanalytic writings than their colleagues in other countries. Conversely, some French psychoanalysts show evidence of existential infiltration into their thinking, despite their explicit and official rejection of existential philosophy.

In some instances psychoanalysis, as it prepared its practitioners to analyze the mind and its pathology and attuned them to probing the psyche, also made them more receptive to phenomenological and existential ideas. In Switzerland, Binswanger, who started as a Freudian and remained Freud's personal friend, discovered Heidegger and then retreated from his Freudian position and developed his *Daseinsanalyse,* a far cry from psychoanalysis. Medard Boss, on the other hand, has been more devoted to Heidegger's thought than Binswanger, whom he criticized for not following Heidegger far enough. Yet Boss has retained closer ties with psychoanalysis, his first love. He underwent a psychoanalysis and thorough psychiatric training, used psychoanalysis in his practice, and is an active member of psychoanalytic societies. Nevertheless, he discarded Freudian theory but retained psychoanalytic techniques.

Some students of both movements have examined them more closely and discovered converging elements in psychoanalytic and existential thought. Studies have appeared on the similarities and parallels in Freud's writings, as well as in those of Adler and Jung, with existentialism. A possibility of a rapprochement between the two movements has been hinted at and discussed. In fact, a reconciliation between existentialism and psychoanalysis has been an explicit intention of some French existential authors. They hoped to achieve perhaps a new and larger conceptual and methodological synthesis with the help of both doctrines. Such a synthesis was one of Paul Ricoeur's aims when he wrote his extensive study, *De l'interprétation: Essai sur Freud* (1965; English translation, *Freud and Philosophy: An Essay on Interpretation,* 1970). Other psychological and psychotherapeutic systems have also been compared with existentialism and found to be congruent in some respects with some existential ideas. Arguments have been proposed, for example, to show that behaviorism can be reconciled with existentialism, and that there is more agreement than opposition between Sartre and Skinner. Kvale and Grenness (1967), after finding basic similarities between Skinner's radical behaviorism and the phenomenology of Sartre and Merleau-Ponty, thought that Skinner's metapsychological views "may be better understood . . . on the basis of Sartre's and Merleau-Ponty's more comprehensive discussions of the philosophical foundations of psychology." These various attempts to examine existentialism in relation to psychoanalysis and behaviorism can be interpreted as an expression of the everpresent search for a synthesis from thesis and antithesis.

A Postscript

An overview of the diverse existential psychotherapies, which usually started with identical common general philosophical assumptions and ended up as complete systems of therapy—diversified, dissimilar, and sometimes in sharp contrast to each other—may leave one perplexed. Even if one succeeds in understanding these different theories and therapeutic approaches—itself not an easy task—one may be at a loss when trying to compare their respective merits and evaluate them. Which is more efficacious, which closer to the truth, which contains in

the balance more valid elements than errors? If one needs psychotherapeutic help, in which therapist's hands would one put onself?
Would one choose the Daseinsanalyse of Binswanger or that of Boss,
the organo-dynamic clinic of Dr. Ey or the psychosynthesis of Dr.
Assagioli, or perhaps undergo logotherapy or the anthropological psychiatric treatment of Gebsattel? And there are still Dr. Laing's therapeutic centers which may be the best place to consider. It is not easy
to determine the value of various psychotherapies because of the lack
of objective rigorous criteria of appraisal. Compare this situation to
judgments of abstract art, where one interpretation of a work may be
just as "correct" as another. It is difficult enough to evaluate psychological hypotheses where at least it is possible to subject them to test-
ing, experimental verification, or logical analysis, but when it comes to
clinical practices and the evaluation of their validity and effectiveness,
the difficulties are compounded. Before some objective criteria of
evaluation are established and applied, individual subjective criteria will
prevail. As to the multiplicity of psychotherapeutic systems, one must
keep in mind the complexities and intricacies of human psychopathology. One can then appreciate the genuine efforts of capable and
sincere men who have groped with compassion and intellectual integrity
for centuries to understand sick minds and thus cure them. We have to
look at these efforts as part of the relentless and arduous pursuit of the
human mind to find itself, to understand itself and the aberrations of
its own and others' minds. These reflections, obviously, apply not
exclusively to existential therapies but to psychoanalytic and other
psychotherapeutic theories and practices as well.

THE EXISTENTIAL IN AMERICAN PSYCHOLOGY

The terms *existential psychology* and *existentialism* were used in
America as early as the beginning of the twentieth century, but in a
meaning entirely different from the present connotation. Titchener
applied these terms to his structural psychology to contrast it with act
and functional psychology. His system of psychology considered contents of consciousness as the subject matter of psychology. The mental
contents were to be studied as bare "existential realities," that is, devoid
of meaning, value, or function, for which reason the adjective "existential" seemed appropriate to Titchener for such a system of psychology.
But "existential psychology" in the present meaning, as previously explained, came to be known in America in the late 1940s as a European
product. The following section will deal with the reactions to and

interpretations of this European existential psychology in America. But first we will comment on William James, whose views some writers find closely resemble existential concepts.

William James as Existentialist

May (1968) has called James a "participant in the existential development." It is easy to see the closeness of James's ideas and emphases to existential thought, especially in his preoccupation with the immediacy of experience and in such concepts as the "stream of consciousness," "union of thought and action," and "will and decision." The existential streak in James is particularly evident in, as May expressed it, James's "humaneness and his great breadth as a human being," which "enabled him to bring art and religion" into his thought "without sacrificing his scientific integrity." As to James's contributions to existential thought, MacLeod (1969) wrote: "My own feeling (or thought) is that Heidegger and Sartre have made no significant contributions to the understanding of human experience that were not anticipated by James." As we look back at the development of American psychology, we see how these existential and phenomenological elements in James's psychology have been ignored or spurned and only its scientific and functional aspects remembered and followed. It took 50 years to rediscover these other aspects.

Introduction of the Existential Approach to America

Translations of existentialist works into English and American studies of the existential movement began to appear in the 1940s. In 1944 Paul Tillich (1886-1965) published an article on existential philosophy. Tillich was born in Germany and resided there until 1933. After he came to the United States, he was a professor of philosophical theology at Union Theological Seminary in New York for 22 years, and from 1955 to 1962 he was a professor at Harvard Divinity School. He then moved to the University of Chicago Divinity School. His numerous books have aroused interest in existential thought and won many sympathizers, especially for existential psychotherapy. He has been a vital link between European and American existential thought.

One early publication, judged by some as the best introduction to existentialism in the English language, was William Barrett's 1947 series of articles "What is Existentialism?," expanded into a book in 1964.

In 1958 Barrett published a study in existential philosophy, *Irrational Man*, which was well received and has been widely read.

As for psychologists or psychiatrists—perhaps because of their long estrangement from philosophy—they at first did not generally show interest in the new philosophical movement and did not see its implications for their domains. What seems to have been psychiatry's first public sign of interest in the movement was the article by H. L. Silverman in the *Psychiatric Quarterly Supplement* in 1947, "The Philosophy and Psychology of Existentialism." This article was highly critical of existentialism.

There were, however, psychologists in America who were familiar with the existentialist movement and whose views were influenced by existential thought. This is shown by the 1950 presentation of a psychological system bearing for the first time the designation "existential." It was *Values and Personality: An Existential Psychology of Crisis* by Werner Wolff (1904-1957). The author was born and educated in Europe, where he became acquainted with existential philosophy. He realized that the existential psychology proposed in his book was only indirectly related to existential concepts, but he felt that the designation "existential" was justified because, as he said, "the frame of reference for this psychological approach is man's existence." He defined existential psychology as being

> man's behavior considered in terms of his individual value system; the psychology of man as far as he questions his existence. Its object is the personal inner experience of the individual; the focus upon the moment when he, consciously or unconsciously, takes his existence into his hands; the focus upon his intent rather than upon his apparent behavior.

One fourth of the book is devoted to the theory of existential psychology, which is contrasted with other theoretical positions in psychology. In this part the author offers a number of novel concepts and postulates related to personality theory. The orientation of the book is clinical, centered around a specific form of neurosis named "existential neurosis" and its therapy. As Wolff relates, he developed the concept of existential neurosis by observing patients whom he treated in the years 1929-1933 in Berlin. Existential neurosis, in his definition, is

> a disturbance of creativeness, that is, of the freedom of self-expression, in whatever area of living caused by an Existential Conflict, which is based upon an individual's direct experience of having lost his connection with the world at large through a disillusion by key figures such as father, mother, beloved, friend.

An "existential conflict" is the conflict experienced by man when he "realizes his freedom of decision and suffers from the burden of his responsibility." The book did not generate much interest among American psychologists. In view of the lack of interest in existentialism here at that time, the message of the book was perhaps too premature to be noticed, much less to generate any discussion.

Existential Analysis in America

At this point something should be said about American psychiatry in relation to European developments. In the 1950s American psychiatrists began to take serious cognizance of European existential analysis. Ulrich Sonnemann's *Existence and Therapy: An Introduction to Phenomenological Psychology and Existential Analysis*—probably the first discussion of European existential psychotherapy in this country—appeared in 1954. The author, a clinical psychologist, born and trained in Europe, has since lectured on and practiced psychotherapy in America. Ideas presented in the book, still relatively foreign here at that time and novel and unorthodox, evidently bewildered a reviewer of this book who confessed that they appeared to him as almost defying "any purely intellectual comprehension" and to be like "double-talk."

Existential analysis eventually found a sympathetic response among psychotherapists and psychiatrists here. The appearance of books and periodicals devoted to existential analysis attests to the existing interest in and support of this new approach to psychotherapy. *The Journal of Existential Psychiatry* (now the *Journal of Existentialism*) appeared in 1960, *The Review of Existential Psychology and Psychiatry* in 1961, *The Existential Analyst,* a newsletter of the New York Institute of Existential Analysis, in 1964, and *Existential Psychiatry* in 1966. In addition, there have been a number of psychiatrists and clinical psychologists in the United States whose viewpoint and practice bear the existential mark. Among them have been Clemens E. Benda, a European-born psychiatrist who had close contact with European existentialists; Bruno Bettelheim, known for his contributions to child psychiatry; Leslie H. Farber, who has shown the importance of studying the will as the prime cause of behavior; C. Gratton Kemp, an exponent of existential counseling; Efren Ramirez, who introduced the existential approach to the treatment of drug addiction; and Thomas S. Szasz, a prolific writer interested in moral and social aspects of psychiatric practice.

An increased interest in the existential approach among American psychiatrists was paralleled by a gradual demise of the influence of psychoanalysis. Psychiatrists Miller, Whitaker, and Fellner (1969), who examined the existential influence upon American psychiatry in the 1950s and 1960s, said that "even though a distinct existential movement has not developed, existential thinkers have contributed substantially to the emerging American psychiatry." They described this new psychiatry as "a composite of traditional psychoanalysis, eclecticism, and hypotheses of existential psychiatry, along with a more delineated appreciation of biological and chemical adjuncts—all cast into a new perspective by the overwhelming spirit for social change which engulfs the world."

Promoters of the Existential Viewpoint

Because of the challenge presented by existential analysis to psychoanalysis, it is not surprising that the first American psychologists who began to study and evaluate the existential movement were clinical psychologists. There had been among them—as well as among personality theorists—some who, independently of European existentialists, were already concerned with existential problems. Finding parallels between existential concepts and their own thinking, they turned to a serious study of the existential movement and by their writings awakened wider interest in it among other psychologists. A prominent role in arousing this interest in existentialism has been played by Rollo May (b. 1909) and Adrian van Kaam (b. 1920).

Rollo May

In 1958 a book appeared, *Existence,* edited by Rollo May and containing his own interpretation of existential thought. This volume was the first sympathetic presentation in America of existentialism as a relevant movement for psychiatrists and psychologists. Although addressed primarily to psychotherapists, the book attracted the attention of many American psychologists. A year later, 1959, a symposium on existential psychology was organized in conjunction with the annual convention of the American Psychological Association in Cincinnati. This was the first time that existential psychology was on the convention's official program. The papers read at this symposium were published in a 1961 book under May's editorship, *Existential Psychology* (2nd ed., 1969). It was hoped, as May said in the foreword, that this book "may serve as a stimulus to students who are interested in the field and that it may suggest topics and questions to be pursued." The contributors to this volume were Gordon Allport, Herman Feifel, Joseph Lyons, Abraham Maslow, and Carl Rogers.

As a clinician and practicing therapist, Rollo May was chiefly interested in the value of the existential approach from the clinical viewpoint, but he viewed this approach from a broader perspective. He confronted it with the prevalent tendencies of contemporary psychology in America. May observes in *Existential Psychology:*

> The existential approach is not a movement back to the armchair of speculation, but an endeavor to understand man's behavior and experience in terms of the presuppositions that underlie them— presuppositions that underlie our science and our image of man. It is the endeavor to understand the nature of this man who *does* the experiencing and to *whom* the experiences happen.

The presuppositions to which May refers here are, in his opinion, of crucial importance for psychology, for they touch upon the most fundamental issue, the nature of man and the nature of his experience. They guide and give meaning to the empirical data gathered in psychology. But this crucial area has almost always been bypassed in psychology. "We tend to assume uncritically and implicitly," he says, "that our particular method is true for all time." May cautions against "absolutizing or dogmatizing" presuppositions. The existential approach calls for a continual analysis and clarification of the basic presuppositions of psychology. He defends the existential approach from the criticism that it is unscientific. He also points out the new dimensions which the existential approach introduces to psychology, its emphasis on will, decision, and problems of the ego. But he also warns about its exaggerations and limitations.

The main theme of May's *Love and Will* (1969), which became a national bestseller and received various awards, is that healthy will depends upon one's capacity to love, and love in turn requires that the individual risk and commit himself—which means the capacity to will. Both love and will depend upon the primordial thrust in life which he calls the daimonic. In *Power and Innocence* (1972) May probed the sources of man's violence and sought to describe the meaning and consequences of the power need which, as he postulated, is basic to every individual.

Adrian van Kaam

Adrian van Kaam has been an active interpreter and exponent of phenomenological-existential psychology. Born in the Netherlands in

1920, he studied philosophy, theology, and psychology in his native country. He subsequently held various teaching and counseling positions. Well acquainted with the European phenomenológical-existential movement, he came to America to continue his studies in psychology. In 1958 he obtained a Ph.D. in psychology at Western Reserve University, and in 1962 he returned to the faculty of Duquesne University, where he founded and directed an interdisciplinary *Institute of Man.* At Duquesne, he has given courses and organized seminars on existential psychology. In addition to teaching, he has lectured extensively on existential psychology in the United States and Canada and has participated in symposia devoted to phenomenology and existential psychology. Having studied in Europe and in the United States, van Kaam has gained familiarity with European as well as American trends and viewpoints in psychology. This familiarity gives him an obvious advantage in promoting the existential approach. He is the author of numerous articles, reviews, and books and is also co-founder and chief editor of *Humanitas,* the journal of the Institute of Man since 1965, and of the *Review of Existential Psychology and Psychiatry.* This review, according to the editorial policy,

> seeks to advance the understanding of human existence by encouraging the dialogue between the behavioral sciences and the phenomenology of man, and to point toward the integration of the theories and data of psychology and psychiatry into a science of man based on increasing knowledge of his essential nature.

By promoting the phenomenological-existential viewpoint in psychology and psychotherapy, van Kaam hopes to expand the horizons of these fields. He does not place himself in opposition to the existing trends, but he would like to add another dimension to bring psychology closer to the ideal of being a true science of man in all his aspects, thereby augmenting the old with the new. Van Kaam calls existential psychology a "scientific theory which attempts to integrate the contributions of the various behavioral sciences." This integration, he believes, cannot be achieved without a comprehensive conceptual framework concerning the nature of man. Such a framework is provided by existential philosophy. However in accepting this framework, a psychologist is not concerned with its ontological or epistemological aspects, nor does he have to presuppose the scientific validity of its concepts. These existential concepts serve him as "hypothetical constructs from which testable propositions can be deduced and put to the empirical test." If they do not pass this test, they are to be dismissed and other propositions are formulated. "The ultimate criteria of existential psy-

chology," van Kaam says, "are the results obtained by strict observation
and research by different specialists in the various areas of psychology.
. . ."

Van Kaam's most significant book is *Existential Foundations of
Psychology* (1966), a re-evaluation of contemporary psychology and an
argument for a new "anthropological psychology" which would assimilate the traditional views and methods and integrate them with
existential ideas. Man constantly evolves in knowledge and experience,
says van Kaam, and psychology must follow this evolution and remain
in harmony with it. His anthropological psychology is to be this kind,
as it strives to integrate all the contributions to the understanding of
man into a comprehensive theory of man. Van Kaam provisionally
defined anthropological psychology as "an open, personal, progressive
integration of the historical and contemporary psychological knowledge
about man—in the light of a phenomenological explication of the
fundamental psychological structure of his personality—in order to
understand his psychology."

Status of Existential Psychology

While it would be interesting to have a detailed survey of opinions
and reactions among contemporary American psychologists, various
publications, papers, and utterances at psychological meetings indicate
that the opinions about existential psychology range over a wide
spectrum. Critics of the existential approach object to its obscure
thought and even more obscure language, its exaggerated subjectivism,
its dogmatic tone, and its unscientific character. Sympathetically disposed psychologists see in existential concepts and theories a new
challenge and a valuable potential for enriching the whole of psychology.
This does not mean that they uncritically accept all existential notions.
On the contrary, they too have reservations about some features of the
existential movement. There are no American psychologists, it appears,
who are entirely committed to one particular existential system or to
existentialism in general. The prevailing tendency seems to be eclectic—
that is, to extract only certain elements from the varieties of existential
thought and perhaps synthesize them with other theories, rather than
to subscribe to a single existential system. One aspect of existential
psychology, however, seems to have met with wide approval among
favorably disposed American psychologists—namely, its decisively
humanistic orientation.

In an article in the *American Psychologist* in 1960, Lawrence A.
Pervin (b. 1936) outlined some of the basic elements of existentialism

and gave his evaluation of the new trend. While he thought that it would be "fool-hardy to accept or reject" existentialism and existential analysis "in their entirety," he admitted that they are potentially useful and "worthy of serious attention and investigation." The article concluded: "They represent possible suggestions for further study by psychology. If approached in this light, I think that existentialism may have much to offer and psychology considerable to gain."

The existential approach has gained the support of several prominent psychologists as well as that of a substantial segment of the younger generation. Inspection of the *Psychological Abstracts* confirms this trend by the evidence of a steady flow of literature on existential topics. Among the well-known American psychologists who aligned themselves in the past with the existential viewpoint and lent it their support were Gordon Allport, Abraham Maslow, Rollo May, as we have already seen, and Carl Rogers.

Abraham Maslow (1908-1970) expressed the feeling of perhaps many American psychologists when he posed the question "What's in existential psychology for us?," which was the title of his paper presented at the A.P.A. symposium in 1959 and published in the book *Existential Psychology* (May, 1969). In this paper he expressed the belief that existential psychology would enrich psychology and that "it may also be an additional push toward the establishment of another *branch* of psychology, the psychology of the fully evolved and authentic self and its way of being." Maslow is discussed more fully in the following chapter.

Gordon W. Allport (1897-1967) became acquainted with phenomenology, it will be remembered, during his studies in Germany, where he experienced the impact of psychologists such as Stumpf, Wertheimer, Köhler, Spranger, William Stern, and Heinz Werner. Later (1953), when he distinguished between the Lockean and the Leibnitzian philosophical traditions in psychology, he placed Husserl and phenomenology in the Leibnitzian tradition. He voiced his opinion about existentialism on several occasions. He thought that existentialism "prepares the way (for the first time) for a *psychology of mankind.*" He explained this notion in the following statement taken from *Existential Psychology* (1969):

A series of facts unites mankind—all mankind. The human being is born of a father and mother, ordinarily conceived and nurtured in love. He pursues certain biological goals; but he also pursues other goals which require him to establish his own identity, to take responsibility, to satisfy his curiosity concerning the meaning of life. He usually falls in love and procreates. He always dies alone. Along the way, he experiences anxiety, longing, pain, and pleasure.

Thomas F. Pettigrew, Allport's former student and now professor of social psychology at Harvard, referred to Allport's influence by saying, "American interest in existentialism would surely have come about if Gordon Allport had never lived. But at least Gordon was responsible for it appearing a little earlier. For example, he introduced existential psychologist Victor Frankl to this country" (Evans, 1970, p. 133). Over 300 Ph.D.'s obtained their degrees during Allport's 18 years as chairman of the Department of Social Relations at Harvard. In 1963, 55 of his Ph.D.'s held a gathering in honor of their mentor and presented him with two bound volumes of their own writings. Among his doctoral students were the distinguished psychologists Jerome Bruner, Hadley Cantril, Gardner Lindzey, Thomas Pettigrew, Leo Postman, Fillmore Sanford, Brewster Smith, and Philip Vernon. This list in itself testifies to the wide circle of Allport's influence.

Carl Rogers (b. 1902) aligned himself, as he said, with those psychologists in America who "are concerned with the whole spectrum of human behavior and that *human* behavior is, in some significant ways, something more than the behavior of our laboratory animals." At the 1963 symposium on "Behaviorism and Phenomenology," he said that the phenomenological-existential view in psychology "carries with it a new philosophical underpinning for psychological science, which is, I believe, more fruitful and more human than the presently held philosophies."

There are psychologists who do not agree with the opinions cited above. They are skeptical of the value of the existential approach; indeed, they perceive in it dangers for psychology. Sigmund Koch (b. 1917), for example, speaking at the symposium in 1963, said that he is somewhat worried "by the style of the current interest in existentialism in American psychology." It seems to him that there is

a disposition to accept in advance an intellectual object the properties of which have hardly been cognized. And there are indications that existentialism is tending to be viewed, in some global sense, as an *external source of authority* for whatever ideas the viewer already owns that he feels to be unconventional.

Koch added:

If existential philosophy is to be of concrete significance for the problems of a psychology of experience, this remains to be *established.* The slogans per se (e.g., "existence precedes essence") are not especially illuminating, whatever comfort they may give. My guess, though limited by very slight contact with existentialist literature, is that even if the conditions for *responsible* exploitation were met, there might not be a great contribution to psychology forthcoming.

Murphy and Kovach (1972), in their *Historical Introduction to Modern Psychology,* observed:

Academic psychology has shown great reserve in response to almost all new "schools" of thought suspected of having philosophical pretensions. Yet for vitality, and for sheer volume of thinking, clinical practice, and research, the newer existentialist, phenomenological, and humanistic psychologies . . . need to be noted here.

CONCLUSION

In the 1960s the existential movement gained a number of capable young proselytes, especially in clinical and counseling psychologies. It was not so much any particular existential philosophy that attracted them but rather the general existential outlook, themes, and clinical practice, and also, in a large degree, the aura of prominent successful American and European clinicians—Binswanger, Frankl, Straus, and May. What Leona Tyler (1971) said of herself is perhaps characteristic of many clinicians. She said, "I would not really call myself an existentialist, and yet some concepts and assumptions derived from this philosophy form the core of my thinking about counseling and many other things." A first serious attempt to construct a comprehensive clinical psychology on existential principles is Ernest J. Keen's work, *Three Faces of Being: Toward an Existential Clinical Psychology* (1970). A characteristic mark of this work, as with other American formulations based on existential thought, is an effort to scoop the best and most suitable—and also perhaps the most intelligible and palatable—products of existentialism and to interweave them together with ideas from other sources, whether Freud, Sullivan, or Laing. Another feature of American works like Keen's book is resistance to accepting any one conception or formula, resulting in freedom from enslavement to one system or person.

SUMMARY

Existential psychology grew out of two philosophical movements, phenomenology and existentialism. In the first part of this chapter the main features of existentialism as a philosophy are sketched, and its founders and leading representatives are introduced. In the second part, the effect of existential thought on psychiatry, psychotherapy, and particularly psychology is pointed out. We outlined the character of existential psychology by specifying its presuppositions, aims, themes, and methods. In reviewing the reactions of American psychology to existential psychology, we cited opinions and attitudes found here. In closing the chapter, we considered the prospects of existential psychology becoming the "Third Force" in American psychology. The following is a brief recapitulation of the main points discussed in the text.

Existential Philosophy

Founder: Søren Kierkegaard (1813-1855)

Chief representatives: In Germany: Martin Heidegger (b. 1889) and Karl Jaspers (1883-1969); in France: Gabriel Marcel (b. 1889) and Jean-Paul Sartre (b. 1905).

Definition: Since existentialism comprises various disparate philosophies with few common characteristics and an extensive range of themes, any brief definition cannot be but a gross oversimplification. In this oversimplified sense, existential philosophy is to be thought of as a movement composed of various philosophies which rest on similar foundation, primarily phenomenological, and which share the same object of inquiry, that is, *existence* as a peculiarly human mode of being. Its focus is on man and his subjective consciousness of being-in-the-world.

Existential Psychology

Definition: Not a school or system, existential psychology declares itself as a new approach and attitude which seeks to complement other trends in psychology. Its basic presuppositions about the nature of psychology and its orientations have been inspired by existential philosophy. Its *aim* is to understand man in his total existential reality, especially in his subjective relationship to himself, to his fellow men, and to the world. It employs all *methods* available, particularly, however, the phenomenological method as the most appropriate one in the exploration of the individual's inner experience. But it also endeavors to develop new methods suited for its areas of investigation. Existential psychology originated in Europe in the 1940s. It began to be studied and discussed in America in the 1950s.

Developments in America:

The first *system of psychology* based on existential principles was proposed by Werner Wolff (1904-1957) in 1950.

The book *Existence,* edited by Rollo May (b. 1909), appeared in 1958.

The first *symposium* on existential psychology was held at the annual meeting of the American Psychological Association in 1959. Papers presented at this symposium were published in book form in 1961, under the title *Existential Psychology,* with Rollo May as editor.

SUGGESTED READINGS

See the bibliography for complete information about the books mentioned here.

On Existentialism, see:

Historical: Spiegelberg (1971)
Philosophy: Barrett (1958, 1964), Olson (1962), Wild (1959)
Readings: Friedman (1964), Kaufmann (1956), Solomon (1972)

On Existential psychology, see

Historical: Spiegelberg (1972a)
Theory: May (1968, 1969), Pervin (1960), Strasser (1965), Van Kaam (1966)

On Existential psychotherapy, see:

Theory and practice: Allers (1961), Keen (1970), Lyons (1963), May (1958), Sonnemann (1954), Van den Berg (1955)
Existentialism and psychoanalysis: Bieliauskas (1964), Ruitenbeek (1962)

5

Humanistic Psychology

In the previous chapters we have reviewed two philosophical movements, phenomenology and existentialism, and their impact on psychology in Europe and America. These movements appealed to that segment of American psychology which was dissatisfied with, or alienated from, behavioristic psychology and psychoanalysis, and which sought an alternative in psychology whose focus would be man and his existential characteristics. This segment responded sympathetically to phenomenology and existentialism and was ready to absorb from them philosophical ideas and concepts, as well as methodological approaches which suited its own theoretical and practical proclivities. As a result of these developments and other forces, a new movement gradually evolved in America and began to grow and become increasingly evident. Although composed of many heterogeneous intellectual strains, this stream shared two basic characteristics: dissatisfaction with the prevailing behavioristic orientation of contemporary psychology, and the intention to make the study of man, his nature, and his existence the focal point of psychology. This movement has come to be identified as *humanistic psychology*.

In this chapter we shall attempt to describe humanistic psychology, its meanings and goals, and to identify its chief exponents and their contributions. The authors feel that the confrontation of the two approaches—humanistic and behavioristic—will be a significant part of the American psychological scene in the future and that therefore students should be alerted to and prepared for the issues which will be debated. Moreover, humanistic psychology merits attention because it is a movement that has inherited at once mentalistic, phenomenological, and existential elements which behaviorism and psychoanalysis have ignored or rejected.

ORIGINS AND GROWTH

Humanistic psychology is not new, original, or unique in focusing on the study of human experience and the human person. Its deep concern with the human being depends perhaps more on philosophy, religion, literature, and the whole long and varied history of humanism than on traditional psychology.

Antecedents

In the German-speaking world for almost a century, there has been a continuing protest against the reduction of psychology to the status of a natural science. In previous chapters we have already referred to the intentionality of Brentano and Husserl and to the symbolism of Cassirer, as distinctively human and as inside processes worthy of investigation by those who would study man. Another of Wundt's contemporaries, Wilhelm Dilthey (1833-1911), called for an understanding or cultural science psychology which emphasized the dynamic nature and unique growth of each individual. He argued that explanatory or natural science psychology was inadequate to understand man. With its atomistic character, laboratory psychology could not perceive man as a whole. Dilthey's disciple, Eduard Spranger, using intuitive rather than laboratory methods, studied the personality of the individual as a whole in relation to his historical environment and his goals and values. As a result of their researches, the Würzburg School under Oswald Külpe demonstrated the non-quantifiable character of thought processes. One member of that school, Karl Bühler, insisted that these processes could not be explained as mere reactions to external stimuli and emphasized the goal-directed and creative nature of thought. In a similar vein, the Gestalt psychologists— Wertheimer, Köhler, and Koffka—stressed the value of phenomenological introspection and linked it with objective experimentation in tneir holistic approach to man. All of these early German investigators recognized an internal human dimension with which, they affirmed, psychological science had to reckon.

Early American advocates of what is today called humanistic

psychology were William James (1842-1910) and G. Stanley Hall (1844-1924). Both wanted a scientific psychology that would restore and preserve the whole man. They believed that psychology should probe the rich affective life that underlies intellect in order to understand man's essential humanity. Both James and Hall viewed with concern the mechanomorphic model of man being forged by the scientific psychology of their day. Later, in the 1930s, Gordon Allport and Henry Murray became ardent proponents of humanistic theories of personality. In the following decade Carl Rogers, the founder of client-centered or non-directive therapy, published *Counseling and Psychotherapy* (1942), and Abraham Maslow published the first account of his theory of motivation (1943). However, these Americans were crying in the wilderness, as their views of man were far removed from the mainstream of American psychology. In America, behaviorism ruled supreme for the first half of the twentieth century. To be a humanistically oriented psychologist before 1950 was tantamount to being ostracized professionally.

Emergence of Humanistic Psychology

Humanistic psychology, as a formal movement, began in the United States and Europe in the 1950s and has been growing steadily in numbers and influence ever since. It was born out of dissatisfaction with the course which psychology had followed in the early twentieth century. This dissatisfaction referred especially to the image of man which modern psychology had constructed, an image which was considered partial, incomplete, and one-sided. It was felt that psychology, particularly behavioristic psychology, became "dehumanized"—that, although spectacularly successful in certain areas, it failed to contribute much to the understanding of man and his existential condition. In fact, it robbed man of his essence.

In the midst of the dissatisfaction with behavioristic psychology, during the 1950s isolated books and papers emphasized the person-centered, the value-centered, the phenomenological, and the existential. Among the significant publications were Maslow's paper on the criteria of the self-actualizing person (1950), his *Motivation and Personality* (1954), Allport's *Becoming* (1955), Moustakas' *The Self* (1956), and Gardner Murphy's *Human Potentialities* (1958). British interest was also evidenced by the appearance of Cohen's *Humanistic Psychology* (1958). In 1954 the Budapest-born psychologist and philosopher of science, Egon Brunswik (1903-1955), a student of Karl Bühler's and then professor of psychology at the University of California at Berkeley, exhorted psychology to emancipate itself from the nomothetic-reductionist natural sciences and to align itself with statistical disciplines with which it seems to have a structural affinity. In the mid-fifties cries were also heard from outside psychology urging psychologists to re-examine their orientation. In an address at the 1955 American Psychological Association Convention, the eminent physicist Robert Oppenheimer warned psychologists not to model their science after an outdated physics and pleaded for pluralism in methodology which would include naturalistic and descriptive methods. Heeding these admonitions, humanistic psychologists have sought to turn the tide toward the "humanization" of psychology. Their emphasis is on man's spontaneity, internal locus of control, uniqueness, and existential problems.

Another factor contributing to the emergence of humanistic psychology was the conviction shared by a number of psychologists that psychology had for too long studied functions of man while consistently missing man himself; that it had concentrated on the secondary and peripheral, while neglecting the primary and the essential. B. Berelson and G. A. Steiner in *Human Behavior: An Inventory of Scientific Findings* (1964) admit, after having reported 1,045 scientific findings about human behavior, that the image of man as it emerges from these findings is "incomplete." They say:

> Indeed, as one reviews this set of findings, he may well be impressed by another omission perhaps more striking still. As one lives life or observes it around him (or within himself) or finds it in a work of art, he sees a richness that somehow has fallen through the present screen of the behavioral sciences. This book, for example, has rather little to say about the central human concerns: nobility, moral courage, ethical torments, the delicate relation of father and son or of the marriage state, life's way of corrupting innocence, the rightness and wrongness of acts, evil, happiness, love and hate, death, even sex.

Humanistic psychology is a reaction against this state of affairs and the psychology responsible for it. It is a countermovement against that dominant psychology, characterized as mechanistic, reductionistic, "ratomorphic," or as "robot psychology," which has reduced man, to use Bugental's (1967) phrase, "to a larger white rat or a slower computer." It also opposes the restrictive methodology which excludes inner experience. As such, humanistic psychology has brought together psychologists representing different and sometimes divergent currents and trends, who agree only on the rejection of the mechanomorphic psychology and on the acceptance of the humanistic denominator; that is, on the concept of man as a creative being, controlled not by outside or unconscious forces but by his own values and choices. In 1958 Abraham H. Maslow called this movement "the Third Force," a designation which has enjoyed popularity and wide use, but which now is a somewhat overworked metaphor. Maslow was called the founder of humanistic psychology, although he himself said in 1970 that humanistic psychology "is the work of *many* men," that it has "no single leader, no one great name by which to characterize it." Among the many from whom it took its inspiration were Erich Fromm, Kurt Goldstein, Karen Horney, Gordon Allport, and Henry Murray.

Humanistic psychology, then, is a product of many individual efforts and an assimilation of many ideas, especially of phenomenological and existential thought. It is a development, however, which is not unique to psychology, but is an expression of a wider, new world-view, a part of a universal humanistic trend manifesting itself in the social sciences, education, biology, and philosophy of science. It is a segment of a larger movement purporting to do justice to man's humanity and—to borrow M. Brewster Smith's (1969) expression— to build "a science *of* man that is *for* man, too."

Development of Humanistic Psychology

The first general outline of humanistic psychology was expressed by Maslow in 1954 in a heading on his mailing list reading: "People who are interested in the scientific study of creativity, love, higher values, autonomy, growth, self-actualization, basic need gratification. . . ." The first public "manifesto" of humanistic psychology in America was an address entitled *Humanistic Psychology: A New Breakthrough,* presented to the Orange County (California) Psychological Association in 1962 by James F. T. Bugental and published in the *American Psychologist* in 1963. But at that time there already existed the *Journal of Humanistic Psychology* (established in 1961) and the American Association for Humanistic Psychology (founded in 1962—now an international organization, the Association for Humanistic Psychology).

In England, John Cohen, professor of psychology at the University of Manchester, disavowed the existing orientation of present-day psychology, especially its reductionism, and called for a reorientation of psychology in his book, *Humanistic Psychology* (1958). As he summarized his position, "the subject matter of psychology is distinctively human; it is not the 'mere lining of physiology.' Our first step should therefore be to study what is characteristic of man, the blossom rather than the root."

In Germany, Albert Wellek, former professor of psychology and director of the Psychological Institute at the University of Mainz, consistently emphasized the humanistic elements in his writings, especially in the field of personality, where his main contributions lie.

In America, the humanistic movement found support at first among psychotherapists, clinical psychologists, and psychologists interested in personality theory, but it gradually won adherents in other circles, academic and experimental. Maslow's humanistic thesis, which, he said, appeared to him at first as "an argument within the family of psychologists," turned out to be "a new general comprehensive philosophy of life," a "humanistic *Weltanschauung*" that attracted a considerable number of psychologists. The publication of a book of readings, *Humanistic Viewpoints in Psychology* (1965), edited by F. T. Severin, helped the humanistic cause considerably by furthering its conceptualization. Other publications, textbooks of general psychology and special studies based on the humanistic viewpoint, appeared in the 1960s. The election of Maslow to the presidency of the American Psychological Association in 1968 was a sign that humanistic themes, as supported by him, gained recognition and respect among American psychologists. By 1970 humanistic psychology had sufficient support within the American Psychological Association to warrant the approval of a Division of Humanistic Psychology (Division 32). Its stated purpose is "to apply the concepts, theories, and philosophy of Humanistic Psychology to research, education, and professional applications of scientific psychology." A clinical psychologist, Carmi Harari, was chosen as the first president of the new division when it was formally organized in 1971.

In 1970, the Association for Humanistic Psychology convened the First International Conference on Humanistic Psychology in Amsterdam, Holland. A second international conference was held in Würzburg, Germany in 1971. The humanistic movement owed much of its organizational coherence and impetus to the energy and enthusiasm of a clinical psychologist, James F. T. Bugental (b. 1915), the first president of the American Association for Humanistic Psychology (1962-1963), who authored *Search for Authenticity* (1965) and edited *Challenges of Humanistic Psychology* (1967).

Abraham H. Maslow

A realistically oriented personality theorist, Abraham H. Maslow (1908-1970) has been regarded as the spiritual father, foremost theoretician, builder of the humanistic orientation and movement, and its most articulate spokesman. It was particularly his persistent affirmation of man's uniqueness and self-actualization that epitomized the humanistic orientation best. Because of his important role in humanistic psychology, it is not surprising that we make frequent references to him and to his formulations in this presentation of humanistic psychology.

Well-trained in experimental psychology and rigorous scientific methodology—training to which he remained faithful—Maslow first studied monkeys under Harry Harlow and wrote his doctoral thesis on the sexual and dominance characteristics of monkeys. Initially, as he related, he was "sold on Behaviorism" and enthusiastic about it, but later "could not stomach it anymore." Eventually he devoted his life to seeking a comprehensive theory of human behavior based on factual evidence, acceptable and useful to all mankind.

Maslow taught at Brooklyn College in New York (1937-1951) before joining the Brandeis University staff in 1951. At Brandeis he was Philip Meyers Professor of Psychology and, from 1951 to 1961, chairman of the psychology department. In 1969 he became Resident Fellow at the W. Price Laughlin Foundation in Menlo Park, California, where he died in 1970. A much published author, Maslow was a founding editor of the *Journal of Humanistic Psychology* and the *Journal of Transpersonal Psychology,* in addition to serving on the editorial boards of 14 other scholarly journals. He wrote several books, some of which have been translated into Italian, Japanese, Polish, and Spanish. Among his best known and most widely read volumes are *Toward a Psychology of Being* (1962; 2nd ed., 1968) and *Motivation and Personality* (1954; 2nd ed., 1970). The former book presents Maslow's psychology of being, which is largely a development of Kurt Goldstein's conception of self-actualization. The work has been hailed as having "a constant optimistic thrust toward a future based on the intrinsic values of humanity." Maslow views man's inner nature as either positively good or neutral, not inherently evil. What is called evil behavior, he claims, is most often a secondary reaction to frustration of this inner nature.

Although Maslow studied and discussed many theoretical and methodological problems of psychology, he is best known for his theory of motivation. In *Motivation and Personality,* which synthesizes three approaches—holistic, motivational, and cultural—he presents his metamotivation theory which concerns itself chiefly with growth motivation. He described six degrees of need priorities which lead to psychological health: physiological needs, safety needs, belongingness needs, love needs, self-esteem needs, and the highest, self-actualization needs. In moving through this hierarchy, man's satisfaction of one drive propels him on to the next. In his researches employing qualitative and observational methods, Maslow has focused principally on the normal or healthy personality. To him normality is a question of self-fulfillment. Neurosis is a blockage of the path to self-actualization. The depth and breadth of Maslow's investigations with regard to man's existential problems have no parallel in American psychology since James.

As to the character of psychology, Maslow (1957) cited a number of specific "musts" which he felt "are essential if psychology is to mature as a science and accept its full responsibilities." Maslow's summarized requirements for future psychology include the notions that:

> Psychology should be more humanistic, that is, more concerned with the problems of humanity, and less with the problems of the guild. . . .
>
> Psychology should turn more frequently to the study of philosophy, of science, of aesthetics, and especially of ethics and values. . . .
>
> American psychology should be bolder, more creative; it should try to discover, not only to be cautious and careful in avoiding mistakes. . . .
>
> Psychology should be more problem-centered, and less absorbed with means or methods. . . .
>
> Psychology ought to become more positive and less negative. It should have higher ceilings, and not be afraid of the loftier possibilities of the human being. . . .
>
> Psychology should study the depths of human nature as well as the surface behavior, the unconscious as well as the conscious. . . .
>
> Academic psychology is too exclusively Western. It needs to draw on Eastern sources as well. It turns too much to the objective, the public, the outer, the behavioral, and should learn more about the subjective, the private, the inner, the meditative. Introspection, thrown out as a technique, should be brought back into psychological research. . . .
>
> Psychologists should study the end experiences as well as the means to ends—the pragmatic, the useful, and the purposive. What does man live for? What makes living worthwhile? What experiences in life justify the pains of existence?
>
> Psychology should study the human being not just as passive clay, helplessly determined by outside forces. Man is, or should

be, an active autonomous, self-governing mover, chooser and center of his own life. . . .

Intellectuals tend to become absorbed with abstractions, words and concepts, and to forget the original real experience which is the beginning of all science. In psychology, this is a particular danger. . . .

The 'lessons of Gestalt psychology and of organismic theory have not been fully integrated into psychology. The human being is an irreducible unit, at least as far as psychological research is concerned. Everything in him is related to everything else, in greater or lesser degree. . . .

Psychologists should devote more time to the intensive study of the single unique person, to balance their preoccupation with the generalized man and with generalized and abstracted capacities. . . .

Finally, as we begin to know more about legitimate wants and needs for personal growth and self-fulfillment, that is, for psychological health, then we should set ourselves the task of creating the health-fostering culture. . . .

As to psychology's responsibility, Maslow said in the same article:

I believe that psychologists occupy the most centrally important position in the world today. I say this because all the important problems of mankind—war and peace, exploitation and brotherhood, hatred and love, sickness and health, misunderstanding and understanding, happiness and unhappiness—will yield only to a better understanding of human nature, and to this psychology alone wholly applies itself.

CHARACTERISTICS OF HUMANISTIC PSYCHOLOGY

There is no conclusive definition of humanistic psychology. The movement can be viewed as both a protest and a new program, even as a new school and a system. Its protest is directed against the entire orientation of psychology since Hobbes and Locke, against its Newtonian and Darwinian models of man, and against its mechanistic, deterministic, and reductionist character. While both Freudism and behaviorism emphasize man's continuity with the animal world, humanistic psychology pays special attention to characteristics and capacities which make man uniquely different from the animals. It is the protest more than specific theories that has attracted, under the banner of humanistic psychology, psychologists who are loosely connected ideologically. The Association for Humanistic Psychology lists four characteristics of most of those who subscribe to the humanistic orientation:

> A centering of attention on the experiencing person and thus a focus on experience as the primary phenomenon in the study of man. Both theoretical explanations and overt behavior are considered secondary to experience itself and to its meaning to the person.

> An emphasis on such distinctively human qualities as choice, creativity, valuation, and self-realization, as opposed to thinking about human beings in mechanistic and reductionistic terms.

> An allegiance to meaningfulness in the selection of problems for study and of research procedures, and an opposition to a primary emphasis on objectivity at the expense of significance.

> An ultimate concern with and valuing of the dignity and worth of man and an interest in the development of the potential inherent in every person. Central in this view is the person as he discovers his own being and relates to other persons and to social groups.

Although these are common elements, the protagonists of humanistic psychology differ widely among themselves. They are far from unanimous. In 1967 Bugental, an enthusiastic leader of the movement, was still able to say, "humanistic psychology is as much distinguished by what it is not or by what it opposes as by what it affirms."

The positive conceptual core and the postulates of humanistic psychology are elusive because of the above-mentioned ideological heterogeneity of this movement, which Maslow (1969) for this reason described as "a coalescence into a single philosophy of various splinter groups in psychology." The essence of this philosophy, as delineated by Maslow, lies in the convictions that: the human species possesses characteristics and capacities which are unique; there are universal ultimate values which are part of man's biological nature—instinctive, not acquired; the ultimate goal of all man's pursuits is self-realization or self-actualization—that is, full use and exploitation of all one's potentialities and capabilities. All these characteristics of human nature can be scientifically established and validated, and having demonstrated these qualities, humanistic psychology may be able to offer a solution to problems which have plagued man for centuries, or may at least help man in his self-realization and thus contribute to his psychological health.

Basic Concepts and Ultimate Goal

An international leader in humanistic psychology as well as a senior spokesman for the movement in America is German-born Charlotte Bühler (b. 1893), wife of the well-known Karl Bühler. Her interest in humanistic psychology dates back to her early career as professor of psychology at the University of Vienna (1922-1938), where she conducted her life-cycle studies as a means of understanding the human being as a whole. In recognition of her contributions to the field, she was named president of the First International Conference on Humanistic Psychology held in Amsterdam in 1970. There she delivered an address on "Basic Theoretical Concepts of Humanistic Psychology," which she further elaborated in her book, *Introduction to Humanistic Psychology,* co-authored with Melanie Allen in 1972.

Charlotte Bühler has consistently reaffirmed the following characteristics of humanistic psychology as the basic ones: striving "to find access to the study and understanding of the person as a whole" (such understanding "requires and implies the knowledge of his whole life history"); close relationship with existentialism as the underlying philosophical basis, and particularly with the experience of intentionality as the "core of a person's self and of his motivation"; preoccupation with the healthy person's end goal of life; and that the most central concept of man is creativity. Humanistic psychology is particularly relevant and important, in her opinion, for psychotherapy and education.

The ultimate goal of humanistic psychology, as seen by Bugental (1967), is "a complete description of what it means to be alive as a human being." This goal, which is not "likely ever to be fully attained," includes a description of man's native potentialities—his growth, maturity, and decline, his interaction with physical and social environment, the range and variety of his experience, and his place in the universe.

Although some humanistic psychologists perceive themselves as opposed to behaviorism and psychoanalysis, Maslow (1969) thought of humanistic psychology as "a larger superordinate structure" which can accommodate behaviorism, psychoanalysis, and other positions in psychology. Maslow was against dichotomies—pro-Freudian or anti-Freudian, pro-behavioristic or anti-behavioristic. He said of himself, "I am Freudian and I am behavioristic and I am humanistic. . . ."

George A. Kelly (1969) expressed a similar view when he said, "It is incredible that humanistic psychology should allow itself to stand opposed to the study of behavior; . . . what now separates humanism from behaviorism . . . is that behavior is more to be used than explained. Indeed what best explains behavior is what it does, just as what best explains man is what he does. So the humanist asks what behavior can do."

Applications

Humanistic psychology not only recognizes the spirit of man and his need to fulfill himself and find meaning in his life, but it also asserts that each person is the most responsible agent in his own life. On that account its principles have implications for ethics (Kurtz, 1969), religion (Hammes, 1971), and the law (Stone, 1971). Thus the tenets and principles of humanistic psychology invite a broad spectrum of application.

Humanistic psychologists have tried to spread their message to men everywhere in the community. They have attempted to apply their principles chiefly to education, business, and psychotherapy. Maslow's dream was the creation of a synergic or, as he later called it, a Eupsychian society where people would cooperate to their mutual advantage and where they could develop their potential and satisfy their psychological needs without restricting others' freedom. In other words, the blueprint of humanistic psychology's program has been the creation of the good society which is fulfilling and renders self-actualization possible.

A prime requisite for the creation of the good society is, obviously, sound education. In *Psychology and the Human Dilemma,* Rollo May (1967) refers to the school as a primary source of learned anxiety and disappointment in the growing person. His educational values are imposed from without by parents and school authorities, not chosen by him. Humanistic psychology rejects the blind authority and competitiveness of traditional education and substitutes internal development and self-reinforcement. It shifts the focus of education to the growth potential of the learner and his human need for self-actualization. Essentially, humanistic psychology's program has demanded reforms in the traditional thinking and training of teachers and school administrators as well as modifications in methods of instruction. Although much has been written about the existential-humanistic perspective in education and its key role in shaping the future of American education, only meager beginnings have been made in instituting the humanistic orientation in American schools up to now. Willis Harman (1971), a well-known Stanford educator, predicts that an individual educated within the humanistic orientation will "become authentically man."

Since in the good society human beings must also work, humanistic reforms are required in business and industry. Maslow himself participated in this sphere of application of humanistic psychology. In *Eupsychian Management* (1965), he described his theory of management which assumes the existence of higher needs and of potential meta-needs in all employees, no matter what their intellectual level. Maslow's management program aimed to establish a democratic boss-worker relationship with an appeal to the highest human motives. Its goal was a work situation in which self-actualization and personal growth would be made possible. In several corporations where Maslowian principles were implemented, notable success was reported in terms of increased employee happiness, efficiency, and productivity, as well as management satisfaction with the program. These results bear testimony to the humanistic conviction that the highest levels of efficiency can only be attained by recognizing the need for self-actualization in every human being.

The applications of humanistic psychology to psychotherapy via the group movement have probably been the most extensive, intensive, varied, and popular. They have also probably been the most controversial aspect of the entire humanistic movement. For this reason they are treated in the separate section which follows.

THE ENCOUNTER GROUP MOVEMENT

Perhaps in no other area has humanistic psychology influenced human lives more than in group techniques designed to facilitate growth and self-realization. In the decades following World War II, these techniques emerged as a new cultural and therapeutic development in the form of intensive group experiences or basic encounter groups. "Encounter," says Burton (1969a), "represents existentialism—the philosophy of the human condition—carried into the corpus of society."

The term *encounter* has been variously used to designate different types of human contact—good, bad, and indifferent. It has been applied to a love relationship between two persons as well as to confrontation with the truth. Generally the term is used today in reference to the convening of a group of persons who, in the course of building relationships with one another, will learn how personality is formed, how it functions, changes, and grows.

Origins and Development

In America, the conceptual framework for these group methods derived principally from Lewinian and Rogerian theories, although Gestalt therapy, with its ideal of present-centeredness, and some varieties of psychoanalysis also contributed. Originally the protagonist of non-directive therapy with a one-to-one relationship of therapist and client, Carl Rogers gradually became the exponent of the group-centered humanistic approach. A noted theorist of the self, Rogers has regarded as universal the need for self-understanding and for building an adequate self capable of establishing satisfying and mutual social relationships. He deemed the encounter process salutary and educational for normal persons as well as for those requiring psychotherapy.

In Europe during the 1950s, considerable theoretical interest in encounter evolved. Ludwig Binswanger, Hans Trüb, Frederick J. J. Buytendijk, and Walter von Baeyer explored the nature and types of encounter between human beings and especially the interpersonal relationship between therapist and client. Analyzing encounter within a biological and psychological framework, Buytendijk argued that for encounter to occur there must be spirit (Geist) present in one man's body and in the body of another. This reciprocal presence renders language and dialogue possible, and only in such mutual communication can encounter be fully realized.

During the late 1960s, a wave of enthusiasm for encounter arose in the United States and abroad. Encounter groups spread rapidly, as did similar groups such as T groups (for Training) and sensitivity groups. Many of these groups were conducted in so-called growth centers, one of the best known in the United States being the Esalen Institute in Big Sur, California. Large numbers of individuals—students, educators, businessmen, executives, delinquents, criminals, drug addicts, the young and old, men and women, married, widowed, divorced, and single—have convened in groups of eight to twenty persons for several hours of a day or evening. Occasionally such groups meet for more extended periods in a prolonged encounter, such as marathon groups. Some groups are leaderless; others are led by trained psychotherapists. More often the groups are led by leaders trained in the social and behavioral sciences than in psychiatry or psychoanalysis. The groups engage in various activities, games, and conversation which facilitate interaction of their members with overt displays of approbation, criticism, affection, warmth, and hostility rather than with the usual tact and restraint that characterize people's behavior in ordinary social situations. In other words, the encounter group strives to create an atmosphere of support and trust in which its participants can unveil the masks that they characteristically wear in public, thereby ventilating their true feelings and sentiments. It thus seeks to enable the participants to become experiencing persons capable of choice, creativity, valuation, and self-actualization.

The idea of the encounter group is similar to that of client-centered therapy, which assumes that an individual can grow in a positive direction if he can liberate himself sufficiently from artificial restraints to see his real, unique, phenomenal self and to interact with other people openly and honestly. It is, therefore, not surprising that the originator of client-centered therapy, Carl Rogers, has become an important leader and professional spokesman for the encounter group movement. His experiences with and views on encounter have been presented in his book, *Carl Rogers on Encounter Groups* (1970). Among others who have contributed significantly to encounter's theory and practice are J. F. T. Bugental, Charlotte Bühler, and Sidney Jourard. Through their contributions they have tried to make humanistic psychology become a reality for people rather than a mere ideological trend described in professional books and journals.

Appraisal

With the rapidly burgeoning development of the encounter group movement, certain features of it have stirred controversy and provoked criticism. Humanistic psychologists themselves have differed concerning the goals of the new techniques. As Bühler and Allen (1972) observed, "The here-and-now experience became a slogan for many of the participants in the group movement and led to an emphasis—and later to an absolute concentration—on the encounters themselves." Some participants who have explored the here-and-now want to go beyond personal fulfillment in a transpersonal direction. Several contemporary leaders of the encounter movement, including Rogers, Greening, Jourard, and May, who heartily endorsed the existential approach, have expressed concern about the various fads this approach has generated. Many encounter groups have practiced eccentric, unconventional, and revivalist modes of behavior.

In 1967, Rogers called attention to possible disadvantages and risks inherent in the group process. He cited, for example, that behavioral changes, if they do occur, may not endure. He admitted that there was a risk—although minimal—that an intensive group experience could be damaging. The surfacing of previously undisclosed tensions was cited as a possible, occasional, unpleasant after-effect. Difficulties were also described as arising from affectional responses, often with a sexual component, stimulated among group members. And yet, Rogers (1969) has called the encounter group "the most important social invention of this century." Similarly, Burton (1969a) sees encounter groups as a means of making the insights and techniques of curative psychotherapy available to every man and not simply to disturbed individuals. Although they have become a means of promoting the existence of the healthy, Burton nevertheless warns that "encounter now desperately requires a scientific basis" as well as theoretical clarification. While staunchly supporting intensive group experiences, Rogers (1970) has called for research, especially of the "natural laboratory" type, in order that group process may be better understood. The encounter movement is satisfying societal needs and reaching many more people than one could have ever anticipated. But Rogers fears that in spite of the demand, if there is no adequate understanding and evaluation of group procedures, their value may be obscured and suppressed by a troubled, irate society.

One of the most successful therapists in the encounter movement, Sidney Jourard, author of *The Transparent Self* (1971), insists that man has a need to make himself known to his fellow man. He has developed a theory that self-knowledge and dynamic relationships are constructed on self-disclosure. On the other hand, Solomon (in Litwak, 1972) has questioned the operating assumption in many encounter groups that "more and more self-disclosure is necessary or good." Many participants have also complained that after the release of feeling and self-disclosure, crucial problems remain.

The question of whether or not encounter groups provide effective therapy remains a debatable issue. At most, all that can be said is that some psychologists agree that these groups are an effective form of treatment for certain problems. Others maintain that the group process has an educational value for participants insofar as it enables them to explore their own potential and life values, to increase their self-awareness, and to come into closer contact with other persons than is ordinarily possible. There are, of course, those psychologists who still regard encounter groups as a fad and as potentially hazardous, in that they may generate acute disturbances in some of their troubled participants. Finally, while conceding that ". . . the group movement is so complex that almost any criticism made about it is going to be valid on some occasion," Greening, in *Existential Humanistic Psychology* (1972), insists that ". . . methods like encounter groups offer a much needed start toward the development of a psychology of whole persons." He also predicts that "when future books on existential and humanistic psychology are written, . . . such groups will be seen even more clearly as a major way in which man makes his own *human* nature."

According to Solomon and Massarik (in Litwak, 1972), the chief need of the encounter movement is standards of performance. Undoubtedly, there are inherent dangers in encouraging undertrained and undersupervised nonprofessionals to employ group interaction procedures indiscriminately. Yet the determination of criteria for measuring effective group work constitutes an urgent, thorny problem. While observing that "the academic degree is often irrelevant," Solomon asks how, with the diversity of philosophies in the field, one can tell who is doing a decent job. In spite of the risks involved, however, both Solomon and Massarik agree that it is necessary to remain experimental. In a similar vein, Murphy and Kovach (1972) conclude that the encounter group

> . . . and the whole conception of group therapy are loosely defined in the humanistic movement. Like all enthusiastic movements, it is still hard to define especially with respect to the limits of classification and the rubrics within which psychologists are to be placed.

Regardless of the need, importance, and potential benefits of the encounter movement, it would seem an exaggeration if the thrust of humanistic psychology were spent on, or exclusively identified with, this movement. It appears that to some the theoretical and investigative ambitions of humanistic psychology are secondary to the activities and practices such as group therapies and encounter sessions.

EVALUATION

Humanistic psychology has been variously described: as a "vigorous," "viable" movement; a "wave of the future" (Rogers, 1967); "a legitimate and hopeful feature of the permanent landscape of psychology" (Matson, 1967); a "bold movement that is spreading like a religion across the U.S. and colonizing Europe" (*Psychology Today,* August 1970); even a movement "capable of changing the course of world history" (Goble, 1970). Some consider humanistic psychology a new philosophy of science. Madsen (1971), whose main work has been the comparative study of psychological theories, wrote:

> After some doubts and ambivalent attitudes toward humanistic psychology, I am now convinced that it represents a new and broader philosophy of science, and that humanistic psychology shares in a "revolution" in the philosophy of science with other philosophical trends of European origin.

On the other hand, there are critics—some very bitter—of humanistic psychology. Maslow (1970) himself admitted that humanistic psychology is "being strained by its own inner dynamics," and he was not certain whether the word "humanistic" will stick for "this all-embracing synthesis and for all its separable aspects." Some critics view the movement as a fad, slogan, or rallying cry rather than a real force. They think of it as an inconsequential and weak movement because it is woven by too many, too divergent, and sometimes even clashing strands, incapable therefore of sustained collaborative action and durable impact. Others have serious doubts about the scientific character of humanistic psychology. M. Brewster Smith (1966) cautioned that humanistic psychology, if it adopts and follows its own concept of science, should

> not lose sight . . . of the important distinctiveness of science as a cultural invention of strategies and institutions that promote cumulative gain in knowledge in a context of free communication, criticism, and replicable observation by qualified members of a scientific community.

S. Koch (1964) voiced his reservations about humanistic psychology, or the "Third Force," at the Rice Symposium. His remarks were summarized in the protocol of the discussion:

> Insofar as he can see, the third force "is an extraordinarily loose congeries of people who are very much concerned about the constriction of problematic interests in American psychology . . . who are eager to embrace some kind of alternative." To speak of "this as a force is the bad use of a metaphor . . . because it is not a third force, it is a group of a large number of individuals who . . . would have considerable difficulty communicating with each other and who stand for nothing focal other than a feeling of disaffection from the emphases of recent American psychology." While he does not reject it, he does not look on it as "some wave of the future" which can "rescue psychology."

There is also the matter of methodology. Does humanistic psychology have adequate methodology—tools, techniques, and procedures—to productively investigate the problems which it ought to investigate on an empirical basis? Humanistic psychologists recognize the importance of a suitable methodology. But it is not enough for humanistic psychology simply to state its case. "Clearly the next step for this psychology and philosophy," wrote Maslow (1970), "is research, research, research—not only in the laboratory but, more importantly, in the field, in society, in factories, homes, hospitals, communities, even nations." Bugental (1967) observed that humanistic psychology "is in the paradoxical position of having at once a tremendous range of available methods for its work and yet a serious methodological problem," which chiefly consists of developing "adequate criteria for evaluating all that is offered." Humanistic psychologists are hopeful that such criteria will be developed, that further productive methods and tools will be available. Two parts of the *Challenges of Humanistic Psychology* (1967)—approximately 140 pages—were devoted to "research areas and methods" and to "research products." Kelly stressed the need for experimental research and appropriate technology for humanistic psychology in his 1966 article, *Humanistic Methodology in Psychological Research* (reprinted in 1969). "This is crucial," he wrote, "humanistic psychology needs a technology through which to express its humane intentions. Humanity needs to be implemented, not merely characterized and eulogized." With regard to Skinner, whom Kelly described as the "currently popular whipping boy for humanistic psychologists," he said, "It is not that man is what Skinner makes of him, but rather that what Skinner can do man can do—and more. Skinner's subjects are not the model of man; Skinner is."

In commenting on a kind of conceptual confusion "all too typical of writings in humanistic psychology," Royce (1972) cautioned that "the present conceptual foundations (logical, linguistic, epistemological) of humanistic psychology are in serious need of diagnosis and repair." There is danger, and there are serious indications of it, that humanistic psychology—instead of concentrating on the consolidation of its conceptualization and on "research, research, research"—may spend its energy and enthusiasm on various novel, perhaps ephemeral, enterprises related to encounter groups, sensitivity training, various group therapies, and fizzle out in this precarious domain. Apparently Maslow (1969) was aware of this danger when he said that some humanistic psychologists "hover on the edge of antiscience and even antirational feelings in their new enthusiasm for 'experiencing.'" A past president of the Association for Humanistic Psychology, Fred Massarik laments (in Litwak, 1972) that "the overcommitment in the experiential direction has produced a growing tide of anti-intellectualism in our movement. There is too much of the attitude, 'All you gotta do is feel.' "

Six years after his previously quoted remarks, Koch (1969) wrote about humanistic psychology's pursuit of various forms of group therapies. He alluded to his experiences at various meetings of the Association for Humanistic Psychology. Thus he concluded that humanistic psychology, which started as a revolt "against nearly a century of prejudged Millian hypothesis (that methods of physical science should be extended to social sciences) and 50 years of reductive behaviorism," achieved "in no time at all . . . a conception of human nature so gross as to make behaviorism seem a form of Victorian sentimentality." Several members of the humanistic movement have publicly expressed concern over some exaggerations and anarchistic and anti-intellectualistic elements of its subgroups; they have also worried about the "increasing slippage" between the idealism of humanistic psychology and reality. Whatever the significance of these symptoms, they tend to alienate some psychologists from the movement and make many others suspicious.

In a more constructive vein, Heinz Ansbacher (1971), an Adlerian and a humanistic psychologist, has suggested that the humanistic movement as it has developed could profit from Adler and his emphasis on social interest. Concerning humanistic psychology, Ansbacher said:

> By its emphasis on the self and absence of the concept of social usefulness, it has recently tended to attract self-seeking groups to the dismay of its responsible leaders. By adopting the concept of social interest the movement would have a tool to remedy the situation and to find a clearer definition of its purpose and direction.

With the help of more robust theoretical underpinning and a balance between the ideal of self-actualization and social interest, the movement may less likely be mistaken for a cult of the self and more effectively achieve the goals set for it by its well-respected founder and protagonist, Abraham H. Maslow.

SUMMARY

This chapter has presented an account of the antecedents, emergence, and development of humanistic psychology. The basic concepts and characteristics of this new approach to man have been described and evaluated.

Definition: Humanistic psychology is a multifaceted approach to human experience and behavior which focuses on man's uniqueness and his self-actualization. It is for some an alternative and for others a complement to the traditional emphases of behaviorism and psychoanalysis.

Approximate date of origin: 1954

Founders: Abraham H. Maslow (Theory)

> Carl R. Rogers (Personality theory and applications to psychotherapy)
>
> Charlotte Bühler (Applications to counseling and developmental psychology)
>
> James F. T. Bugental (Applications to clinical psychology)

Subject matter of psychology: Man's subjective experience; his uniqueness which differentiates him from the lower animals.

Methods of study: Various methods including interviews, life histories, literary and other creative productions.

Principal areas of interest and research: The normal healthy personality. Motivation, personality, and creativity, especially man's potentialities for growth and how he can achieve his potential. Human values.

Chronology

1954   The first general sketch of humanistic psychology appears as the heading of a mailing list compiled by Abraham H. Maslow: "People who are interested in the scientific study of creativity, love, higher values, autonomy, growth, self-actualization, human need gratification, etc."

1955   The term "humanistic psychology" in its current usage is first used by Hadley Cantril in "Toward a Humanistic Psychology."

1956   Abraham H. Maslow publishes another article also called "Toward a Humanistic Psychology."

1958   *Humanistic Psychology,* a volume by John Cohen, stresses that the subject matter of psychology is distinctively human and that its starting point must be the phenomena of experience. Maslow designates humanistic psychology "the Third Force."

1961   *Journal of Humanistic Psychology* is founded in the United States by Anthony Sutich.

1962   *American Association for Humanistic Psychology* (AAHP) is established.

J. F. T. Bugental presents the first manifesto of humanistic psychology, "Humanistic Psychology: A Major Break-through," to the Orange County (California) Psychological Association.

1965   *Humanistic Viewpoints in Psychology: A Book of Readings,* edited by Frank T. Severin, appears. It is the first American volume presenting the concepts and views of philosophers and psychologists relevant to the humanistic movement.

1970   The American Psychological Association approves the establishment of a Division of Humanistic Psychology (Division 32). First International Conference on Humanistic Psychology is held at Amsterdam, with Charlotte Bühler as president.

1971   Second International Conference on Humanistic Psychology is held at Würzburg, Germany.

Presidents of the Association for Humanistic Psychology

1962-63	James F. T. Bugental
1963-64	Sidney Jourard
1964-65	Edward J. Shoben
1965-66	Charlotte Bühler
1966-67	S. Stansfeld Sargent
1967-68	Jack R. Gibb
1968-69	Gerard V. Haigh
1969-70	Floyd Matson
1970-71	Denis O'Donovan
1971-72	Fred Massarik
1972-73	Lawrence N. Solomon

SUGGESTED READINGS

For a brief survey of the historical roots, goals, methodology, theoretical bases, and applications of humanistic psychology, the reader should see:

Bühler, C., & Allen, M. *Introduction to humanistic psychology.* Monterey, California: Brooks/Cole, 1972.

A comprehensive array of the protests of humanistic psychology against behavioristic psychology and of the aspirations of this new approach to man may be found in:

Severin, F. T. (Ed.) *Humanistic viewpoints in psychology: A book of readings.* New York: McGraw-Hill, 1965, and in a revision: Severin, F. T. (Ed.) *Discovering man in psychology.* New York: McGraw-Hill, 1972.

A good, general view of the leaders, ideas, methods, and perspectives of humanistic psychology is available in:

Bugental, J. F. T. (Ed.) *Challenges of humanistic psychology.* New York: McGraw-Hill, 1967.

For a complete listing of Abraham H. Maslow's publications see:

Abraham H. Maslow: A bibliography. *Journal of Humanistic Psychology,* 1970, **10,** 98-110.

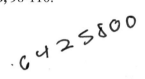

6

A Retrospect and Conclusions

The review of the two new and most powerful philosophical movements of this century and their influence on psychology leads to some reflections and conclusions regarding the relationship between philosophy and psychology, conceptions of psychology, factors which were responsible for the emergence and growth of the "Third Force" in America, and finally the prospects for humanistically oriented psychology. At the end some desiderata will be addressed to the new movement.

Every history contains a lesson to be discovered and learned. Our reflections, gleaned from the historical panorama just reviewed, are presented here with this thought in mind. Since they came from viewing different foci of this panorama, they do not have the continuity and structure of a discourse. They are, moreover, expressed as suggestions, probings, and questions rather than as categorical statements. Their telegraphic format is a deliberate time and space saving device.

PHILOSOPHY AND PSYCHOLOGY

There is no escape from philosophy. The question is only whether a philosophy is conscious or not, whether it is good or bad, muddled or clear. Anyone who rejects philosophy is himself unconsciously practicing a philosophy.

—Karl Jaspers, *Way to Wisdom*

1. The separation of psychology from philosophy at the end of the nineteenth century as the condition for psychology's independence as a science and the subsequent deliberate aphilosophical orientation of American psychology in the first part of this century have not prevented philosophy—particularly the phenomenological and existential philosophy—from affecting modern psychological thought and methodology. While in the nineteenth century empirical philosophy and, to a lesser degree, Kantian philosophy provided the philosophical substructure for psychology, in this century thus far no other philosophical movement has had more profound influence on psychology than phenomenology and existentialism. Are these philosophical influences "passing episodes" in the history of psychology, or merely "local or national reactions and not universal or universalizable," as Jean Piaget (1965) described them? Only the future will tell.

2. In the meantime, increasing contacts between psychology and philosophy and a growing appreciation of mutual benefits arising from a philosophico-psychological dialogue have developed. Philosopher Ernest Nagel (1965) has observed that: "psychologists are compelled by developments in their science to come to grips with problems that have a philosophical dimension, as well as that philosophers who are seeking to interpret various forms of human experience in a responsible manner cannot safely ignore pertinent aspects of psychology." It is recognized that, as psychologist Stephen Winokur (1971) put it, "espousal of any position, whether it be behavioristic or mentalistic, is a metascientific activity which belongs to philosophy proper." It appears that while at one time liberation from philosophy was a condition for the progress of psychology, today psychology's progress is conditioned by its contact with philosophy.

3. American psychologists, responding to phenomenology and existentialism, have been characteristically selective and eclectic in assimilating ideas from these movements and reluctant to commit themselves to any one particular system. They tended to shun heavy philosophizing and to appropriate only those ideas which were readily intelligible and workable. The positivistic thinking, pragmatism, and aphilosophism, to which most American psychologists have been exposed in their training, perhaps had something to do with this tendency. Humanistic psychology appears to be a product of a selective incorporation and interweaving of many philosophical and cultural elements into one structure. A harmonious integration of so many and varied elements will be a serious task for the humanistic movement and a likely condition for its effectiveness.

DIFFERENT CONCEPTIONS OF PSYCHOLOGY

1. Phenomenology's infiltration into psychology raised the question of whether phenomenological psychology had the proper credentials to be considered a science on a par with the psychology modeled after physics, which led to a dichotomous view of science. The dichotomy of sciences was strongly advocated at one time in Germany by Dilthey and others in their well-known distinction between *Naturwissenschaften* and *Geisteswissenschaften,* or natural and humanistic sciences. Arguments for a similar distinction have been advanced in America by theoreticians concerned with the scientific status and legitimacy of the phenomeno-logical-existential approach in psychology.

2. The history of psychological schools and movements reveals that their underpinning is a specific concept or model of man and his nature. As Carl Rogers said, "each current of psychology has its own implicit philosophy of man." This philosophy dictates theoretical stand, goals, and methods of the current. Thus, while one concept of man may lead to a psychology which seeks to manipulate man, another may postulate freedom and self-realization of man as the principal goal of psychology.

3. The new trends discussed in this book can be perceived in a larger historical context—as a continuation and recent expression of a trend which began a hundred years ago with Brentano and James, and which grew through the work and thought of various thinkers: Husserl, Dilthey, Jaspers, the Würzburg and Austrian schools, and Bergson and existentialism in France. This trend can be contrasted with the current, also steadily gaining in strength and numbers, which began with Wundt and was gradually built into a most powerful psychological formula by Watson, Pavlov, Piéron, and Skinner and, from the philosophical side, by logical positivism and operationism. This picture is a gross over-simplification, but it can designate the polarization that is well acknowl-edged in psychology. Will the two orientations—one like a small David challenging mighty Goliath on the psychological arena—coexist in peace or must they struggle for power in the psychological kingdom? What-ever their future position, clashes appear inevitable, since these positions have implications for man as an individual, and human values are at stake. These clashes may be healthy for psychology and perform the function described by Alfred N. Whitehead, who said, "A clash of doctrines is not a disaster—it is an opportunity. . . . The clash is a sign that there are wider truths and finer perspectives. . . ." William McDougall had a similar thought in 1932 with respect to the division of psychological schools at that time:

This state of affairs has many drawbacks; but it has, I hold, this advantage: the great issues in dispute, if they are sharply pointed up, stimulate the student to think and challenge him to strive toward decisions while, at the same time, he gets a glimpse of the extent of our ignorance and of the magnitude of the tasks that lie before us. So treated, psychology, as a provocative to thinking, has, it seems to me, no rival among the academic disciplines.

4. The humanistic movement reflects the growing concern among scientists about the place of human values and social responsibility in their structure and activities. Psychologists feel more and more that psychology's most important task is to understand the human condition, identify its ills, and counteract tendencies which threaten complete dehumanization of man. Probably this consideration of man's plight and the activities stemming from it will be a salient feature of some segment of American psychology in the 1970s. In this context, one may envision a polarization between those who subscribe to man's freedom, dignity, and the preservation of those ideals, and those who hold them as fictions to be abandoned. This polarization can be tied historically to the polarization described above.

THE THIRD FORCE REVISITED

1. The term *Third Force* is by now a somewhat overworked term. We are in need of a more precise collective term for all the nonbehavioristic and nonpsychoanalytic alternatives, including phenomenologically, existentially, and humanistically oriented psychologies.

The rise of the Third Force has been an interesting historical phenomenon in American psychology. Three major factors have contributed to its emergence and proliferation: (1) immigration of scholars from Europe in the 1930s and after World War II; (2) receptivity of American psychology and support from influential figures such as Allport, MacLeod, May and Rogers; and (3) the leadership, writings, and activities of Abraham Maslow.

2. The immigration of European philosophers and psychologists— mostly refugees from Hitler's oppression—affected American psychology in many substantial ways. Conversely, the contact with America had an effect on the immigrants, their views, productivity, and reaction to European philosophy. The greatest psychological brain power came to America from the German-speaking countries, and much less from other lands. It would be valuable to have an accurate and full

picture and documentation of the intellectual ties between American psychology and European movements during years 1930-1950.

3. Would we have the Third Force without the influx of so many intellectuals from Europe? Could that movement have emerged spontaneously? There are reasons to believe, considering the massiveness of the intellectual onslaught in a short space of time, that the immigration at least greatly accelerated its rise.

It must be also remembered that without the receptivity of American psychologists, the Third Force could not flourish. The phenomenological-existential movement in America encountered a favorable confluence of ideological and social conditions. Rapid technological changes, the growing alienation of man in a highly industrial society, the fresh memory of the cruelties of the war, the threat of nuclear destruction, together with the increasing disavowal by some psychologists of the prevailing robot (von Bertalanffy) and ratomorphic (A. Koestler) type of psychology prepared a fertile ground for the seeds from which the Third Force grew. One also has to consider the sympathetic and sometimes enthusiastic reception by prominent psychologists who independently developed ideas akin to those advocated by the European thinkers. Moreover, there was the characteristic American intellectual curiosity to know and understand novel ideas, which helped the assimilation of European thought.

4. Abraham Maslow, himself an intriguing historical phenomenon on the American scene, worthy of careful analysis by historians of psychology, played a key role in the Third Force, as we have seen. His vast research program—still awaiting implementation—should keep psychologists busy for decades. In the meantime, it is clear that his thought is gaining popularity and acceptance not only in America but also in Europe and Asia. His books are being translated into foreign languages and the number of books about him and his psychology has been growing.

5. Will the Third Force, and American humanistic psychology in particular, become a force in Europe and have any impact on European psychology? Will there be a repetition of the history of experimental psychology, which was first imported from Europe and once developed into a large academic field in America, exerted in turn a considerable influence on European psychology? There are signs, such as the two international meetings of humanistic psychology in Holland and Germany, that the American movement will be echoed in Europe.

6. Some desiderata expressed in current literature with regard to the Third Force allow us to see what features of this movement are considered most desirable. They can be briefly summarized:

(a) Avoidance of disunity and striving for a larger perspective, encompassing many viewpoints.

(b) Less protestation and rhetoric, more solid research and positive productivity.

(c) Generation of testable hypotheses and workable reliable methods of investigation.

(d) Continuous dialogue with other psychological orientations and systems.

(e) Overcoming the often-criticized provincialism and ethnocentrism of American psychology, becoming familiar with developments abroad, continuous communication with psychological and philosophical thought abroad, and frequent personal contacts with the *Kulturträgers* of the world. Why should we wait for another catastrophe before we meet the intellectual cream of other countries?

Gardner Murphy (1969) who, as a historian and author, has surveyed the American and world psychological scenes for the last 50 years, had this to say about the human predicament:

The year 2000 can come, and the twenty-first century can offer less terror and more joy, but only if psychologists have learned both *how to look inside* and *how to look outside;* how to recognize the reciprocities of inner and outer, through methods that are as far-ranging and as deeply human as is the human stuff that is being studied.

BIBLIOGRAPHY

To facilitate finding references, letters have been placed in the left margin: **E** for Existential, **G** for General, **H** for Humanistic, and **P** for Phenomenological entries.

E   Allers, R. *Existentialism and psychiatry.* Springfield, Ill.: Charles C Thomas, 1961.

G   Allport, G. W. *Becoming.* New Haven: Yale, 1955.

G   Allport, G. W. *Personality and social encounter.* Boston: Beacon Press, 1960.

G   Allport, G. W. Autobiography. In E. G. Boring, & G. Lindzey (Eds.), *A history of psychology in autobiography.* Vol. V. New York: Appleton-Century-Crofts, 1967.

E   Allport, G. W. Comment on earlier chapters. In R. May (Ed.), *Existential psychology.* (2nd ed.) New York: Random House, 1969.

H   Ansbacher, H. Alfred Adler and humanistic psychology. *Journal of Humanistic Psychology,* 1971, **11**, 53-63.

G   Arnold, M. B. *Emotion and personality.* New York: Columbia University Press, 1960. 2 vols.

E   Assagioli, R. *Psychosynthesis.* New York: Hobbs, Dorman, 1965.

H   Back, K. *Beyond words.* New York: Russell Sage Foundation, 1972.

P   Bannister, D., & Fransella, F. *Inquiring man: The theory of personal constructs.* Baltimore: Penguin Books, 1971.

P   Bannon, J. F. *The philosophy of Merleau-Ponty.* New York: Harcourt, Brace & World, 1967.

E   Barrett, W. *Irrational man: A study in existential philosophy.* New York: Doubleday, 1958.

E   Barrett, W. *What is existentialism?* New York: Grove Press, 1964.

E   Benda, C. E. Existentialism in philosophy and science. *Journal of Existential Psychiatry,* 1960, **1**, 284-314.

G   Berelson, B., & Steiner, G. A. *Human behavior: An inventory of scientific findings.* New York: Harcourt, Brace & World, 1964.

G   Berlyne, D. E. American and European psychology. *American Psychologist,* 1968, **23,** 447-452. Also in V. S. Sexton, & H. Misiak (Eds.), *Historical perspectives in psychology: Readings.* Belmont, Cal.: Brooks/Cole, 1971.

E   Bieliauskas, V. J. Existential philosophy and psychoanalysis. In R. W. Russell (Ed.), *Frontiers in psychology.* Chicago: Scott, Foresman, 1964.

137

E   Binswanger, L. *Being-in-the-world.* New York: Harper Torchbooks, 1968.

E   Bixler, J. S. The existentialists and William James. *American Scholar,* 1959, **28,** 80-90.

G   Bocheński, I. M. *Contemporary European philosophy.* (Trans. from German by D. Nicholl and K. Aschenbrenner) Berkeley: University of California Press, 1961.

G   Boring, E. G. *A history of experimental psychology.* (2nd ed.) New York: Appleton-Century-Crofts, 1950.

P   Brody, N., & Oppenheim, P. Tensions in psychology between the methods of behaviorism and phenomenology. *Psychological Review,* 1966, **73,** 295-305.

P   Brody, N., & Oppenheim, P. Methodological differences between behaviorism and phenomenology. *Psychological Review,* 1967, **74,** 330-334.

G   Brunswik, E. Historical and thematic relations of psychology to other sciences. *Scientific Monthly,* 1956, **83,** 151-161. Also in V. S. Sexton, & H. Misiak (Eds.), *Historical perspectives in psychology: Readings.* Belmont, Cal.: Brooks/Cole, 1971.

H   Bugental, J. F. T. Precognitions of a fossil. *Journal of Humanistic Psychology,* 1962, **2,** 38-46.

H   Bugental, J. F. T. Humanistic psychology: A new break-through. *American Psychologist,* 1963, **18,** 563-567.

H   Bugental, J. F. T. The third force in psychology. *Journal of Humanistic Psychology,* 1964, **4,** 19-25.

H   Bugental, J. F. T. *The search for authenticity: An existential-analytic approach to psychotherapy.* New York: Holt, Rinehart & Winston, 1965.

H   Bugental, J. F. T. (Ed.) *Challenges of humanistic psychology.* New York: McGraw-Hill, 1967. (a)

H   Bugental, J. F. T. The challenge that is man. *Journal of Humanistic Psychology,* 1967, **7,** 1-9. (b)

H   Bühler, C. Some observations on the psychology of the third force. *Journal of Humanistic Psychology,* 1965, **5,** 54-56.

H   Bühler, C. Human life goals in the humanistic perspective. *Journal of Humanistic Psychology,* 1967, **7,** 36-52.

H   Bühler, C. Humanistic psychology as an educational program. *American Psychologist,* 1969, **24,** 736-742.

H   Bühler, C. Basic theoretical concepts of humanistic psychology. *American Psychologist,* 1971, **26,** 378-386.

H   Bühler, C. Autobiography. In L. J. Pongratz, W. Traxel, & E. G. Wehner (Eds.), *Psychologie in Selbstdarstellungen.* Bern: Hans Huber, 1972.

H   Bühler, C., & Allen, M. *Introduction to humanistic psychology.* Monterey, Cal.: Brooks/Cole, 1972.

H   Burton, A. (Ed.) *Encounter.* San Francisco: Jossey Bass, 1969. (a)

E   Burton, A. The authentic person in existential psychology. *Pastoral Psychology,* 1969, **20,** 17-26. (b)

P   Buytendijk, F. J. J. The phenomenological approach to the problem of feelings and emotions. In M. L. Reymert (Ed.), *Feelings and emotions.* New York: McGraw-Hill, 1950.

P   Buytendijk, F. J. J. *Phénomenologie de la rencontre.* Paris: Desclée de Brouwer, 1952. (Originally published: *Eranos Jahrbuch,* 1951, **19,** 431-486.)

P   Buytendijk, F. J. J. Die Bedeutung der Phänomenologie Husserls für die Psychologie der Gegenwart. La signification de la phénoménologie Husserlienne pour la psychologie actuelle. In H. L. van Breda (Ed.), *Husserl et la pensée moderne.* Haag: Nijhoff, 1959.

P   Cairns, D. Results of Husserl's investigations. *Journal of Philosophy,* 1939, **36,** 236-238.

H   Cantril, H. Toward a humanistic psychology. *Etc. A Review of General Semantics,* 1955, **12,** 278-298.

H   Cardno, J. A. Psychology: Human, humanistic, humane. *Journal of Humanistic Psychology,* 1966, **6,** 170-177.

E   Caruso, I. A. *Existential psychology from analysis to synthesis.* (Trans. from the 1951 German edition of *Psychoanalyse und Synthese der Existenz* by Eva Krapf) New York: Herder & Herder, 1964.

H   Chein, I. *The science of behavior and the image of man.* New York: Basic Books, 1972.

H   Child, I. L. *Humanistic psychology and the research tradition: Their several virtues.* New York: Wiley, 1973.

H   Cohen, J. *Humanistic psychology.* London: George Allen & Unwin, 1958.

H   Coleman, J. C. Conflicting views of man's basic nature. In F. T. Severin (Ed.), *Humanistic viewpoints in psychology: A book of readings.* New York: McGraw-Hill, 1965.

G   Collier, R. M. Selected implications from a dynamic regulatory theory of consciousness. *American Psychologist,* 1964, **19,** 265-269.

P   Combs, A. W., & Snygg, D. *Individual behavior: A perceptual approach to behavior.* (Rev. ed.) New York: Harper, 1959.

E   Correnti, S. A comparison of behaviorism and psychoanalysis with existentialism. *Journal of Existentialism,* 1965, **5,** 379-388. Also in V. S. Sexton, & H. Misiak (Eds.), *Historical perspectives in psychology: Readings.* Belmont, Cal.: Brooks/Cole, 1971.

P   Day, W. F. Radical behaviorism in reconciliation with phenomenology. *Journal of the Experimental Analysis of Behavior,* 1969, **12,** 315-328.

EP   Dempsey, P. J. R. *The psychology of Sartre.* Cork, Ireland: Cork University Press, 1950.

G   Donceel, J. F. *Philosophical anthropology.* New York: Sheed and Ward, 1967.

H   Egan, G. *Encounter: Group processes for interpersonal growth.* Belmont, Cal.: Brooks/Cole, 1970.

P   Egan, L. J. Comment on Hitt's analysis. *American Psychologist,* 1970, **25,** 567.

P   Embree, L. E. (Ed.) *Life-world and consciousness: Essays for Aron Gurwitsch.* Evanston: Northwestern University Press, 1972.

E   Erikson, R. W. Some historical connections between existentialism, daseinsanalysis, phenomenology, and the Würzburg school. *Journal of General Psychology,* 1967, **75,** 3-24.

G   Evans, R. I. *Gordon Allport: The man and his ideas.* New York: Dutton, 1970.

P   Farber, M. *The foundation of phenomenology.* (2nd ed.) New York: Paine-Whitman, 1962.

E   Frankl, V. E. *Man's search for meaning: An introduction to logotherapy.* New York: Washington Square, 1963.

E   Friedman, M. (Ed.) *The worlds of existentialism.* New York: Random House, 1964.

P   Gaffron, M. *Die Radierungen Rembrandts, Originale und Drucke.* Mainz: Kupferberg, 1950.

H   Gale, R. *Developmental behavior: A humanistic approach.* New York: Free Press, 1969.

E   Gendlin, E. T. *Experiencing and the creation of meaning.* New York: Free Press, 1962.

P   Gibson, J. J. *The perception of the visual world.* Boston: Houghton Mifflin, 1950.

P   Gibson, J. J. *The senses considered as perceptual systems.* Boston: Houghton Mifflin, 1966.

G   Gibson, J. J. Autobiography. In E. G. Boring, & G. Lindzey (Eds.), *A history of psychology in autobiography.* Vol. V. New York: Appleton-Century-Crofts, 1967.

EP   Gilbert, A. R. Franz Brentano in the perspective of existential psychology. *Journal of History of Behavioral Sciences,* 1968, **4,** 249-253.

P   Giorgi, A. *Psychology as a human science: A phenomenologically based approach.* New York: Harper & Row, 1970. (a)

P   Giorgi, A. Toward phenomenologically based research in psychology. *Journal of Phenomenological Psychology,* 1970, **1,** 75-98. (b)

H   Goble, F. G. *The third force: The psychology of Abraham Maslow.* New York: Grossman, 1970.

P   Goldstein, K. *The organism: A holistic approach to biology derived from pathological data in man.* New York: American Book, 1938. (Paperback published: Boston: Beacon Press, 1963.)

P   Goldstein, K. Autobiography. In E. G. Boring, & G. Lindzey (Eds.), *A history of psychology in autobiography.* Vol. V. New York: Appleton-Century-Crofts, 1967.

H Greening, T. C. (Ed.) *Existential humanistic psychology.* Belmont, Cal.: Brooks/Cole, 1971.

P Grene, M. *Approaches to a philosophical biology.* New York: Basic Books, 1968.

P Groman, W. Comment on "Two models of man." *American Psychologist,* 1970, **25,** 566-567.

P Gurwitsch, A. *The field of consciousness.* Pittsburgh: Duquesne University Press, 1964.

P Gurwitsch, A. *Studies in phenomenology and psychology.* Evanston: Northwestern University Press, 1966.

E Hall, M. H. An interview with "Mr. Humanist" Rollo May. *Psychology Today,* 1967, **1,** 25-29, 72-74.

H Hammes, J. A. *Humanistic psychology: A Christian interpretation.* New York: Grune & Stratton, 1971.

EH Harman, W. W. The future of the existential-humanistic perspective in education. In T. C. Greening, (Ed.), *Existential humanistic psychology.* Belmont, Cal.: Brooks/Cole, 1971.

P Havens, L. Karl Jaspers and American psychiatry. *American Journal of Psychiatry,* 1967, **124,** 66-70.

P Henle, M., & Baltimore, G. Portraits in straw. *Psychological Review,* 1967, **74,** 325-329.

P Hitt, W. Two models of man. *American Psychologist,* 1969, **24,** 651-658.

P Hodges, H. A. (Ed.) *Wilhelm Dilthey: An introduction.* London: Routledge, 1944.

P Hodges, H. A. *The philosophy of Wilhelm Dilthey.* London: Routledge, 1952.

E Holt, H. Ludwig Binswanger (1881-1966)—a tribute. *Journal of Existentialism,* 1966, **7,** 93-96.

P Husserl, E. *Ideas.* (Trans. by W. R. Boyce Gibson) New York: Collier, 1962. (First German edition, 1913; first English edition, 1931.)

P Husserl, E. *Phänomenologische Psychologie: Vorlesungen Sommersemester 1925.* Haag: Nijhoff, 1962.

P Husserl, E. *Phenomenology and the crisis of philosophy.* (Trans. with notes and an introduction by Quentin Lauer) New York: Harper Torchbooks, 1965.

P Ingarden, R. *Time and modes of being.* (Trans. from Polish by H. Micheida) Springfield, Ill.: Charles C Thomas, 1964.

E Jaspers, K. Philosophical autobiography. In P. A. Schilpp (Ed.), *The philosophy of Karl Jaspers.* New York: Tudor, 1957.

E Jaspers, K. *Way to wisdom: An introduction to philosophy.* (Trans. by R. Manheim) New Haven: Yale University Press, 1954.

P Jessor, R. Issues in the phenomenological approach to personality. *Journal of Individual Psychology,* 1961, **17,** 27-38.

P   Johann, R. O. The return to experience. *Review of Metaphysics*, 1963-64, **17**, 319-339.

H   Jourard, S. *The transparent self*. (2nd ed.) Princeton: Van Nostrand, 1971.

H   Jourard, S. *Self-disclosure*. New York: Wiley, 1971.

P   Katz, D. *The world of colour*. (Trans. by R. B. MacLeod and G. W. Fox) London: Kegan Paul, Trench, Trubner, 1935. (First German edition, 1930.)

P   Katz, D. *Gestalt psychology: Its nature and significance*. (Trans. by R. Tyson) New York: Ronald Press, 1950.

P   Katz, D. Autobiography. In E. G. Boring et al. (Eds.), *A history of psychology in autobiography*. Vol. 4. Worcester, Mass.: Clark University Press, 1952.

E   Kaufmann, W. A. (Ed.) *Existentialism from Dostoevsky to Sartre*. New York: Meridian, 1956.

E   Keen, E. J. *Three faces of being: Toward an existential clinical psychology*. New York: Appleton-Century-Crofts, 1970.

E   Keen, E. J. A rapprochement in the psychologies of Freud and Sartre. *The Psychoanalytic Review*, 1971, **58**, 183-188.

P   Kelly, G. A. *The psychology of personal constructs*. New York: Norton, 1955. 2 vols.

H   Kelly, G. A. Humanistic methodology in psychological research. *Journal of Humanistic Psychology*, 1969, **9**, 53-65.

G   Koch, S. Psychology and emerging conceptions of knowledge as unitary. In T. W. Wann (Ed.), *Behaviorism and phenomenology*. Chicago: University of Chicago Press, 1964.

G   Koch, S. Psychology cannot be a coherent science. *Psychology Today*, 1969, **3**, 64-68.

P   Kockelmans, J. J. *Edmund Husserl's phenomenological psychology: A historico-critical study*. Pittsburgh: Duquesne University Press, 1967.

P   Kockelmans, J. J. *A first introduction to Husserl's phenomenology*. Pittsburgh: Duquesne University Press, 1967.

P   Kockelmans, J. J. Husserl's original view on phenomenological psychology. In J. Kockelmans (Ed.), *Phenomenology*. New York: Doubleday, 1967.

P   Kockelmans, J. J. Phenomenological psychology in the United States: A critical analysis of the actual situation. *Journal of Phenomenological Psychology*, 1971, **1**, 139-171.

G   Köhler, W. *Gestalt psychology*. New York: Liveright, 1929.

G   Köhler, W. Value and fact. *Journal of Philosophy*, 1944, **41**, 197-212. Also in M. Henle (Ed.), *The selected papers of Wolfgang Köhler*. New York: Liveright, 1971.

P   Krech, D. Comments. In J. R. Royce (Ed.), *Toward unification in psychology*, Toronto: University of Toronto Press, 1970.

G   Krantz, D. L., Hall, R., & Allen, D. William McDougall and the problem of purpose. *Journal of History of Behavioral Sciences,* 1969, **5,** 25-38.

E   Kronfeld, A. Die Bedeutung Kierkegaards für Psychologie. *Acta Psychologica.* Hague, 1935 **1,** 135-156.

P   Kuenzli, A. E. (Ed.) *The phenomenological problem.* New York: Harper, 1959.

H   Kurtz, P. (Ed.) *Moral problems in contemporary society: Essays in humanistic ethics.* Englewood Cliffs, N.J.: Prentice-Hall, 1969.

P   Kvale, S., & Grenness, C. E. Skinner and Sartre: Towards a radical phenomenology of behavior? *Review of Existential Psychology and Psychiatry,* 1967, **7,** 128-148.

P   Kwant, R. C. *The phenomenological philosophy of Merleau-Ponty.* Pittsburgh: Duquesne University Press, 1963.

P   Landsman, T. Four phenomenologies. *Journal of Individual Psychology,* 1958, **14,** 29-37.

P   Langan, T. Maurice Merleau-Ponty: In memoriam. *Philosophical and Phenomenological Research,* 1962-63, **23,** 205-216.

E   Lapointe, F. H. A bibliography on Jean-Paul Sartre for the behavioral sciences. *Journal of Phenomenological Psychology,* 1971, **1,** 237-261.

EP Lapointe, F. H. Phenomenology, psychoanalysis and the unconscious. *Journal of Phenomenological Psychology,* 1971, **2,** 5-25.

P   Lauer, J. Q. *The triumph of subjectivity: An introduction to transcendental phenomenology.* New York: Fordham University Press, 1958.

E   Lefebre, L. The psychology of Karl Jaspers. In P. A. Schilpp (Ed.), *The philosophy of Karl Jaspers.* New York: Tudor, 1957.

P   Linschoten, H. *On the way toward a phenomenological psychology.* Giorgi, A. (Ed.), Pittsburgh: Duquesne University Press, 1968.

H   Litwak, L. "Rolfing," "Aikido," hypnodramas, psychokinesis, and other things beyond the here and now. *The New York Times Magazine,* December 17, 1972. p. 18.

E   Lowrie, W. *Kierkegaard.* New York: Harper, 1962. 2 vols. (Originally published in 1938.)

G   Lowry, R. Psychoanalysis: The philosophy of physicalism. *Journal of History of Behavioral Sciences,* 1967, **3,** 156-167.

EP Luijpen, W. *Existential phenomenology.* Pittsburgh: Duquesne University Press, 1960.

P   Lyons, J. *Psychology and the measure of man: A phenomenological approach.* Glencoe, Ill.: The Free Press of Glencoe, 1963.

G   Lyons, J. *A primer of experimental psychology.* New York: Harper & Row, 1965.

G   Lyons, J. *Experience: An introduction to a personal psychology.* New York: Harper & Row, 1973.

P   MacLeod, R. B. Phenomenological approach to social psychology. *Psychological Review*, 1947, **54**, 193-210. Also in A. E. Kuenzli (Ed.), *The phenomenological problem*. New York: Harper, 1959.

P   MacLeod, R. B. David Katz. 1884-1953. *Psychological Review*, 1954, **61**, 1-4.

P   MacLeod, R. B. Phenomenology: A challenge to experimental psychology. In T. W. Wann (Ed.), *Behaviorism and phenomenology*. Chicago: University of Chicago Press, 1964.

G   MacLeod, R. B. (Ed.) *William James: Unfinished business*. Washington, D.C.: American Psychological Association, 1969.

G   MacLeod, R. B. Newtonian and Darwinian conceptions of man; and some alternatives. *Journal of History of Behavioral Sciences*, 1970, **6**, 207-218. (a)

P   MacLeod, R. B. Psychological phenomenology: A propaedeutic to a scientific psychology. In J. R. Royce (Ed.), *Toward unification in psychology*. Toronto: University of Toronto Press, 1970. (b)

H   Maddi, S. R., & Costa, P. T. *Humanism in personology: Allport, Maslow, and Murray*. New York: Aldine-Atherton, 1972.

H   Madsen, K. B. Humanistic psychology and the philosophy of science. *Journal of Humanistic Psychology*, 1971, **11**, 1-10.

P   Maher, B. *Clinical psychology and personality: The selected papers of George Kelly*. New York: Wiley, 1969.

G   Mandler, J. M., & Mandler, G. The diaspora of experimental psychology: The Gestaltists and others. In D. Fleming, & B. Bailyn (Eds.), *Perspectives in American history*. Vol. II. Boston: Charles Warren Center for Studies in American History, 1968.

H   Maslow, A. H. A theory of human motivation, *Psychological Review*, 1943, **50**, 370-396.

H   Maslow, A. H. Self-actualizing people: A study of psychological health. *Personality Symposia:* Symposium #1 on Values. New York: Grune & Stratton, 1950.

H   Maslow, A. H. Toward a humanistic psychology. *Etc. A Review of General Semantics*, 1956, **13**, 10-22.

H   Maslow, A. H. A philosophy of psychology: The need for a mature science of human nature. *Main Currents in Modern Thought*, 1957, **13**, 27-32. Also in F. T. Severin (Ed.), *Humanistic viewpoints in psychology*. New York: McGraw-Hill, 1965.

H   Maslow, A. H. *Eupsychian management: A journal*. Homewood, Ill.: Irwin-Dorsey, 1965.

H   Maslow, A. H. *Toward a psychology of being*. (2nd ed.) Princeton: Van Nostrand, 1968.

H   Maslow, A. H. Existential psychology—what's in it for us? In R. May (Ed.), *Existential psychology*. (2nd ed.) New York: Random House, 1969.

H   Maslow, A. H. Toward a humanistic biology. *American Psychologist*, 1969, **24**, 724-735.

H   Maslow, A. H. *Motivation and personality.* (2nd ed.) New York: Harper & Row, 1970.

H   Maslow, A. H. *The farther reaches of human nature.* New York: Viking, 1971.

H   Matson, F. W. *Being, becoming, and behavior: The psychological sciences.* New York: George Braziller, 1967.

H   Matson, F. W. (Ed.) *Without/within: Behaviorism and humanism.* Monterey, Cal.: Brooks/Cole, 1973.

E   Maupin, E. W. Zen Buddhism: A psychological review. *Journal of Consulting Psychology,* 1962, **26,** 362-378.

E   May, R. (Ed.) *Existence: A new dimension in psychiatry and psychology.* New York: Basic Books, 1958.

H   May, R. *Psychology and the human dilemma.* Princeton: Van Nostrand, 1967.

E   May, R. Existential psychology. In *International Encyclopedia of the Social Sciences.* Vol. 13. New York: Macmillan & Free Press, 1968.

E   May, R. *Existential psychology.* (2nd ed.) New York: Random House, 1969. (a)

E   May, R. *Love and will.* New York: Norton, 1969. (b)

E   May, R. *Power and innocence: A search for the sources of violence.* New York: Norton, 1972.

P   McGill, V. J. Behaviorism and phenomenology. *Philosophy and Phenomenological Research,* 1966, **26,** 578-588.

P   Meissner, W. The implications of experience for psychological theory. *Philosophy and Phenomenological Research,* 1966, **24,** 503-528.

P   Merleau-Ponty, M. *Phenomenology of perception.* New York: Humanities, 1962. (First French edition, 1945).

P   Merleau-Ponty, M. *The structure of behavior.* Boston: Beacon, 1963. (First French edition, 1942).

P   Merleau-Ponty, M. *The visible and the invisible.* (Trans. by A. Lingus) Evanston: Northwestern University Press, 1968.

P   Métraux, A. Vision and being in the last lectures of Maurice Merleau-Ponty. In L. E. Embree (Ed.), *Life-world and consciousness: Essays for Aron Gurwitsch.* Evanston: Northwestern University Press, 1972.

G   Metzger, W. The historical background for national trends in psychology: German psychology. *Journal of History of Behavioral Sciences,* 1965, **1,** 109-115. Also in V. S. Sexton, & H. Misiak (Eds.), *Historical perspectives in psychology: Readings.* Belmont, Cal.: Brooks/Cole, 1971.

H   Meyer, D. H. The scientific humanism of G. Stanley Hall. *Journal of Humanistic Psychology,* 1971, **11,** 207-213.

P   Michotte, A. Autobiography. In E. G. Boring, et al. (Eds.), *A history of psychology in autobiography.* Vol. 4. Worcester, Mass.: Clark University Press, 1952.

P   Michotte, A. et al. *Causalité, permanence et réalité phénoménales.* Louvain: Publications Universitaires, 1962.

P   Michotte, A. *The perception of causality.* (Trans. by T. R. and E. Miles) London: Methuen, 1963.

E   Miller, M. H., Whitaker, C. A., & Fellner, C. H. Existentialism in American psychiatry: Ten years later. *American Journal of Psychiatry,* 1969, **125,** 1112-1115.

P   Mischel, T. Merleau-Ponty's phenomenological psychology. *Journal of History of Behavioral Sciences,* 1966, **2,** 172-176.

G   Misiak, H., & Sexton, V. S. *History of psychology: An overview.* New York: Grune & Stratton, 1966.

P   Morrison, J. Husserl and Brentano on intentionality. *Philosophy and Phenomenological Research,* 1970, **31,** 27-46.

H   Moustakas, C. E. (Ed.) *The self: Explorations in personal growth.* New York: Harper, 1956.

H   Murphy, G. *Human potentialities.* New York: Basic Books, 1958.

G   Murphy, G. Psychology in the year 2000. *American Psychologist,* 1969, **24,** 523-530. Also in V. S. Sexton, & H. Misiak (Eds.), *Historical perspectives in psychology: Readings.* Belmont, Cal.: Brooks/Cole, 1971.

G   Murphy, G., & Kovach, J. K. *Historical introduction to modern psychology.* (3rd ed.) New York: Harcourt Brace Jovanovich, 1972.

E   Muuss, R. Existentialism and psychology. *Educational Theory,* 1956, **6,** 135-153.

G   Nagel, E. Psychology and the philosophy of science. In B. Wolman (Ed.), *Scientific psychology,* New York: Basic Books, 1965.

E   Nath, P. Existential trends in American psychology. *Psychologia,* 1963, **6,** 125-130.

E   Nauman, S. E., Jr. *The new dictionary of existentialism.* New York: Philosophical Library, 1971.

P   Nuttin, J. Albert Edouard Michotte van den Berck: 1881-1965. (Trans. by M. D. Boring) *American Journal of Psychology,* 1966, **79,** 331-341.

E   Olson, R. G. *An introduction to existentialism.* New York: Dover, 1962.

P   Paci, E. *The function of the sciences and the meaning of man.* (Trans. by P. Piccone and J. E. Hansen) Evanston: Northwestern University Press, 1972.

E   Pervin, L. A. Existentialism, psychology, and psychotherapy. *American Psychologist,* 1960, **15,** 305-309.

G   Piaget, J. *Insights and illusions of philosophy.* (Trans. by W. Mays) New York: World, 1971. (First French edition in 1965).

G   Piaget, J. Psychology and philosophy. In B. Wolman (Ed.), *Scientific psychology,* New York: Basic Books, 1965.

E   Pilkington, G. W., & Glasgow, W. D. Towards a rehabilitation of introspection as a method in psychology. *Journal of Existentialism,* 1967, **7,** 329-350.

E   Rabil, A., Jr. *Merleau-Ponty: Existentialist of the social world.* New York: Columbia University Press, 1967.

G   Rachlin, H. *Introduction to modern behaviorism.* San Francisco: Coby & Freeman, 1971.

P   Rancurello, A. *A study of Franz Brentano: His psychological standpoint and his significance in the history of psychology.* New York: Academic Press, 1968.

P   *Rencontre, encounter, Begegnung: Contributions à une psychologie humaine dédiés au professeur F. J. J. Buytendijk.* Utrecht: Uitgeverij Het Spectrum, 1957.

G   Reuchlin, M. The historical background for national trends in psychology: France. *Journal of History of Behavioral Sciences,* 1965, **1,** 115-123. Also in V. S. Sexton, & H. Misiak (Eds.), *Historical perspectives in psychology: Readings.* Belmont, Cal.: Brooks/Cole, 1971.

E   Richardson, W. J. *Heidegger: Through phenomenology to thought.* The Hague: Nijhoff, 1963.

E   Richardson, W. J. Humanism and existential psychology. In T. C. Greening (Ed.), *Existential humanistic psychology,* Belmont, Cal.: Brooks/Cole, 1971.

P   Ricoeur, P. *Husserl: An analysis of his phenomenology.* (Trans. by E. G. Ballard and L. E. Embree) Evanston: Northwestern University Press, 1967.

P   Ricoeur, P. *Freud and philosophy: An essay on interpretation.* (Trans. by D. Savage) New Haven: Yale University Press, 1970.

EP   Riese, W. Phenomenology and existentialism in psychiatry: An historical analysis. *Journal of Nervous and Mental Diseases,* 1961, **132,** 469-484.

P   Robinet, A. *Merleau-Ponty, sa vie, son oeuvre avec un exposé de sa philosophie.* Paris: Presses Universitaires de France, 1962.

H   Rogers, C. R. *Counseling and psychotherapy.* Boston: Houghton Mifflin, 1942.

P   Rogers, C. R. Toward a science of the person. In T. W. Wann (Ed.), *Behaviorism and phenomenology.* Chicago: University of Chicago Press, 1964.

H   Rogers, C. R. Some questions and challenges facing a humanistic psychology. *Journal of Humanistic Psychology,* 1965, **5,** 1-5.

H   Rogers, C. R. Some thoughts regarding the current philosophy of the behavioral sciences. *Journal of Humanistic Psychology,* 1965, **5,** 182-194.

H   Rogers, C. R. The process of the basic encounter group. In J. F. T. Bugental (Ed.), *Challenges of humanistic psychology*. New York: McGraw-Hill, 1967.

H   Rogers, C. R. Autobiography. In E. G. Boring, & G. Lindzey (Eds.), *A history of psychology in autobiography*. Vol. V. New York: Appleton-Century-Crofts, 1967.

H   Rogers, C. R. The increasing involvement of the psychologist in social problems: Some comments, positive and negative. *California State Psychologist*, 1968, **9,** 29-31.

H   Rogers, C. R. *Carl Rogers on encounter groups*. New York: Harper & Row, 1970.

H   Royce, J. R. On conceptual confusion in humanistic psychology. *Contemporary Psychology*, 1972, **17,** 704-705.

E   Ruitenbeek, H. M. (Ed.) *Psychoanalysis and existential philosophy*. New York: Dutton, 1962.

E   Ryback, D. Existentialism and behaviorism: Some differences settled. *Canadian Psychologist*, 1972, **13,** 53-60.

P   Sardello, R. J. Behaviorism (versus?) (and?) (or?) phenomenology? *American Psychologist*, 1970, **25,** 567-568.

P   Sartre, J. P. *The emotions: Outline of a theory*. New York: Philosophical Library, 1948.

P   Sartre, J. P. *The psychology of imagination*. New York: Philosophical Library, 1948.

E   Sartre, J. P. *Existential psychoanalysis*. New York: Philosophical Library, 1953.

E   Schilpp, P. A. (Ed.) *The philosophy of Karl Jaspers*. New York: Tudor, 1957.

E   Schrag, O. O. *Existence, Existenz, and transcendence: An introduction to the philosophy of Karl Jaspers*. Pittsburgh: Duquesne University Press, 1971.

H   Severin, F. T. (Ed.) *Humanistic viewpoints in psychology: A book of readings*. New York: McGraw-Hill, 1965.

H   Severin, F. T. (Ed.) *Discovering man in psychology*. New York: McGraw-Hill, 1972.

G   Sexton, V. S., & Misiak, H. (Eds.) *Historical perspectives in psychology: Readings*. Belmont, Cal.: Brooks/Cole, 1971.

E   Silverman, H. L. The philosophy and psychology of existentialism. *Psychiatric Quarterly Supplement*, 1947, **21,** 10-16.

P   Simmel, M. L. (Ed.). *The reach of mind*. New York: Springer, 1968.

P   Smith, K. *Behavior and conscious experience: A conceptual analysis*. Athens, Ohio: Ohio University Press, 1969.

H   Smith, M. B. An ambiguous case for humanistic psychology. *Science*, 1966, **158,** 284-285.

G   Smith, M. B. *Social psychology and human values*. Chicago: Aldine, 1969.

P Snygg, D. The need for a phenomenological system of psychology. In A. E. Kuenzli (Ed.), *The phenomenological problem.* New York: Harper, 1959.

H Solomon, L. M., & Berzon, B. (Eds.) *New perspectives on encounter groups.* San Francisco: Jossey-Bass, 1972.

EP Solomon, R. C. (Ed.) *Phenomenology and existentialism.* New York: Harper & Row, 1972.

E Sonnemann, U. *Existence and therapy: An introduction to phenomenological psychology and existential analysis.* New York: Grune & Stratton, 1954.

P Spiegelberg, H. The relevance of phenomenological philosophy for psychology. In E. N. Lee, & M. Mandelbaum (Eds.), *Phenomenology and existentialism.* Baltimore: Johns Hopkins Press, 1967.

P Spiegelberg, H. *The phenomenological movement: A historical introduction.* (2nd ed.; 3rd impression) The Hague: Nijhoff, 1971. 2 vols.

P Spiegelberg, H. *Phenomenology in psychology and psychiatry: A historical introduction.* Evanston: Northwestern University Press, 1972. (a)

P Spiegelberg, H. What William James knew about Edmund Husserl. In L. E. Embree (Ed.), *Life-world and consciousness: Essays for Aron Gurwitsch.* Evanston: Northwestern University Press, 1972. (b)

P Spranger, E. *Types of men.* (Trans. by P. J. W. Pigors) Halle: Niemeyer, 1928.

E Stone, C. Existential humanism and the law. In T. C. Greening (Ed.), *Existential humanistic psychology.* Belmont, Cal.: Brooks/Cole, 1971.

P Strasser, S. Phenomenological trends in European psychology. *Philosophical and Phenomenological Research,* 1957-58, **18,** 18-34.

P Strasser, S. *Phenomenology and the human sciences.* Pittsburgh: Duquesne University Press, 1963.

P Strasser, S. Phenomenologies and psychologies. *Review of Existential Psychology and Psychiatry,* 1965, **5,** 80-105.

P Strasser, S. *The idea of dialogal phenomenology.* Pittsburgh: Duquesne University Press, 1969.

P Straus, E. W. The primary world of the senses. Glencoe: Free Press, 1963.

P Straus, E. W. *Phenomenology: Pure and applied.* Pittsburgh: Duquesne University Press, 1965.

E Strickland, B. Existential psychology. In G. Powers, & W. Baskin (Eds.), *New outlooks in psychology.* New York: Philosophical Library, 1968.

H Sutich, A. J. Transpersonal psychology: An emerging force. *Journal of Humanistic Psychology,* 1968, **8,** 77-78.

H   Sutich, A. J., & Vich, M. A. *Readings in humanistic psychology.* New York: The Free Press, 1969.

P   Thines, G. The phenomenological approach in comparative psychology. *Journal of Phenomenological Psychology,* 1970, **1,** 63-73.

G   Titchener, E. B. *Systematic psychology: Prolegomena.* Ithaca: Cornell University Press, 1972. (First publication in 1929)

G   Turner, M. B. *Philosophy and the science of behavior.* New York: Appleton-Century-Crofts, 1967.

E   Tyler, L. E. Existentialism in counseling. *The Counseling Psychologist,* 1971, **2,** 30-32.

P   Tymieniecka, A. *Phenomenology and science in contemporary European thought.* Toronto-New York: Farrar, Straus & Cudahy, 1962.

E   Ungersma, A. *The search for meaning: A new approach to psychotherapy.* Philadelphia: Westminster Press, 1968.

P   Van den Berg, J. H. *The phenomenological approach to psychiatry.* Springfield, Ill.: Charles C Thomas, 1955.

EP   Van Kaam, A. L. Assumptions in psychology. *Journal of Individual Psychology,* 1958, **14,** 22-28.

EP   Van Kaam, A. L. *The third force in European psychology—its expression in a theory of psychotherapy.* Greenville, Del.: Psychosynthesis Research Foundation, 1960.

EP   Van Kaam, A. L. The impact of existential phenomenology on the psychological literature of Western Europe. *Review of Existential Psychology and Psychiatry,* 1961, **1,** 63-92.

EP   Van Kaam, A. L. Existential psychology as a comprehensive theory of personality. *Review of Existential Psychology and Psychiatry,* 1963, **3,** 11-26.

EP   Van Kaam, A. L. *Existential foundations of psychology.* Pittsburgh: Duquesne University Press, 1966.

P   Walker, K. F. A critique of the phenomenological theory of behavior. *Australian Journal of Psychology,* 1957, **9,** 97-104.

P   Wann, T. W. (Ed.) *Behaviorism and phenomenology: Contrasting bases for modern psychology.* Chicago: University of Chicago Press, 1964.

P   Watson, R. I. The historical background for national trends in psychology: United States. *Journal of History of Behavioral Sciences,* 1965, **1,** 130-138.

P   Wellek, A. The phenomenological and experimental approaches to psychology and characterology. In H. P. David, & H. von Bracken (Eds.), *Perspectives in personality theory.* New York: Basic Books, 1957.

P   Wellek, A. The impact of the German immigration on the development of American psychology. *Journal of History of Behavioral Sciences,* 1968, **4,** 207-229.

P　Wellek, A. Autobiography. In L. J. Pongratz, W. Traxel, & E. G. Wehner (Eds.), *Psychologie in Selbstdarstellungen*. Bern: Hans Huber, 1972.

P　Wetherick, N. E. Can there be non-phenomenological psychology? *The Human Context*, 1972, **4,** 50-60.

E　Wild, J. *The challenge of existentialism*. Bloomington: Indiana University Press, 1959.

P　Wilshire, B. W. *William James and phenomenology: A study of "The principles of psychology."* Bloomington: Indiana University Press, 1968.

H　Wilson, C. *New pathways in psychology: Maslow and the post-Freudian revolution*. London: Gollancz, 1972.

P　Winokur, S. A review. *Contemporary Psychology*, 1971, **16,** 421.

P　Winthrop, H. Some considerations concerning the status of phenomenology. *Journal of General Psychology*, 1963, **68,** 127-140.

E　Wolff, W. *Values and personality: An existential psychology of crisis*. New York: Grune & Stratton, 1950.

P　Zaner, R. M. Criticism of "Tensions in psychology between methods of behaviorism and phenomenology." *Psychological Review*, 1967, **74,** 318-324.

P　Zaner, R. M. *The way of phenomenology: Criticism as a philosophical discipline*. New York: Pegasus, 1970.

P　Zener, K. The significance of experience of the individual for the science of psychology. In H. Feigl et al. (Eds.), *Minnesota Studies in the Philosophy of Science*. Vol. 11. Minneapolis: University of Minnesota Press, 1958.

P　Zener, K., & Gaffron, M. Perceptual experience: An analysis of its relations to the external world through internal processings. In S. Koch (Ed.), *Psychology: A study of a science*. Vol. 4. New York: McGraw-Hill, 1962.

Name Index

153

Subject Index

159